Becoming Northeast

I0473778

Jason Britt

ISBN: 1478373016
ISBN-13: 978-1478373018

DEDICATION

This book is dedicated to the employees of Northeast Pharmaceuticals and their families. Thank you for all you do. We would not be who we are without your hard work and sacrifice. You are the best and bring out the best in me. I count it a privilege to know you.

CONTENTS

ACKNOWLEDGMENTS

I would like to thank the design team at robinbirdwell.com for their expertise in all things blog and book cover related. Joe and Robin are the best! I love you guys. Also, a big thank you to Steven and Michelle Lambert of michellemariephotography.com. Your work is amazing. I am always in awe when I get my pictures back. Finally, a huge thank you to all of our customers. Your job is a labor of love. Your stories were the inspiration for this work.

Foreword

It takes a lot to build something from nothing. However, I think it takes more courage to take something existing, redefine it, and turn it into something bigger. As we enter our seventh year of business I begin to realize that is exactly what we have done with Northeast. We bought a company with a very limited scope. At the time of our purchase Northeast Pharmaceuticals only served a three county block in Alabama. The customer target was very broad and the vision was very small.

We took ownership and changed all of that. We enlarged the service area and pursued a niche market. We moved into neighboring states with zeal, driven to be the best we could be for our customers. It has been a great ride so far and we look forward to the next turn in the road.

My business partners Daniel and Don Mims are two of the best people on the planet you could go into business with. Daniel and I have been friends since middle school. I learn a lot from his character. He always leans towards grace and mercy; and patience is his hallmark. Don is like a father to me. I have learned a lot about objectivity from him. Don also has an uncanny ability for "getting a read" on people and making connections. It is fun to watch him work a deal. I love and respect them both. I know at the end of the day their friendship and loyalty is solid. I am a lucky guy who could not ask for more. This has been a great adventure for sure.

It has also been a challenging one. We have had to deal with our share of growing pains. Opening new pharmacies is never a fluid process and a myriad of variables always lie in wait to make it stressfully exciting. In fact, as I write this we are in the process of opening yet another pharmacy in Rome, GA. We have already had to wait on certain items before we can give a green light to the contractor for build out to proceed. There is also licensure that must be submitted for processing, various inspections that need to occur, inventory accounts that need to be set up, staff that must be hired/trained, and on and on it goes.

Fortunately for us, this is not our first barbeque. However, there was once a time when it was. Sometimes it went off without a hitch. Other times the horses came unhitched and the wheels fell off the wagon. In the pages that follow, you will be presented with some of those stories. I believe failure is a necessary part of leadership. To only present the successes without giving an honest look at our failures only tells part of the story. At the end of the day it is a false representation of who we are. A lot of blood and sweat has gone into Northeast to make it great, but the picture would be incomplete if the tears were left out.

Finally, the lessons that follow on life and leadership can be taken out of the context of our world and placed in yours. They can be applied to your personal and professional life. All it takes is a decision on your part to act on the concepts. They are simple and timeless. I hope you have as much fun reading these stories as I did writing them.

CHAPTER 1
KNOCK, KNOCK

Nothing could have prepared me for what happened on a nondescript weekday in the summer of 2006. I was sitting at the car wash with my friend Daniel Mims as he hung up the phone. "What was that about?" I quipped. "Two sisters are trying to sell a pharmacy in the Northern part of the state and my name came up. It is probably nothing, but I am willing to take a look and see what they have to offer" he replied. Looking back, sometimes it is the little statements in life that ultimately carry the most gravity. That conversation would hang in the air until November of the same year.

Daniel was already successful in his own right. Two years previously he started a company called Institutional Pharmacy Solutions. That idea was birthed out of the frustration he experienced while working for another long term care pharmacy. That company served the nursing home market at large and did a really good job with it. They had a few clients who were not nursing homes and yet they were trying to fit them into that box. Those clients approached Daniel with their concerns and he came up with an incredible solution. However as it often goes in business, what you see as incredible, corporate sees as tedious, costly, and too much trouble to implement. The short answer... they said no to his idea.

So Daniel did what Daniel does best; he went out on his own and solved their problems. I was invited to come aboard and join the team which then consisted of him, his wife, and myself. I spent the next two years of my life implementing automated systems for small to mid size behavioral health operations across the state. Daniel got the leads and pitched the sale. I would help install the equipment on the back end (with his help initially), and his wife would handle all the billing, licensure, and processing. Business was booming and life was good in our little world. People were starting to take notice and Institutional Pharmacy Solutions was beginning to make a name for itself.

That is why I was really surprised when I found myself in his office one afternoon looking over profit and loss statements for this unknown local pharmacy called Northeast Pharmaceuticals. They were located in the Northeast part of the state in a small town called Gadsden, Alabama and they were a three year old, two person start-up. "Just look over the numbers and tell me what you think", Daniel said. I took a look at their monthly profit and said something to the effect of "Are these numbers real?" We spent the next half hour talking about profit potential and process related issues. I told him it looked like a good buy and he should pursue it, that I would help in whatever capacity he needed me to and I thought that was the end of that. He would buy the pharmacy and I would be there to help.

A few days later we were talking in his office again and he indicated that he was going to purchase the pharmacy. I congratulated him on a good decision only to hear him say the following, "Did I tell you the deal I made with my dad? I told him I would give him 'X' amount of ownership if he came up with 'X' amount of the purchase price". "He would be crazy not to take an offer like that!", I replied. "If that were offered to me I would be all over it!". I never anticipated what would have happened next. Daniel looked at me and said "It's funny you say that because I want to offer you 'X' amount of ownership if you can come up with 'X'".

Without hesitation I asked when he would need it and I left that day with a mission. I had nothing of real value to my name, but I was going to find a way to come up with this money... and I did.

That decision was about one thing, **recognizing opportunity.** Mastering that one skill is essential as a leader and crucial to your personal success. I am a student of Robert Kiyosaki and Donald Trump. I learn a lot from their business acumen and have read most of their books. Kiyosaki uses a phrase often that I love. He says that the rich think differently. They think in terms of risk vs. reward.

This way of thinking is probably very different than the way most of your friends think. Most people make decisions based on factors such as "How much will it cost me?", or "Can I afford to make this decision?". The rich think in terms of "How much do I stand to gain?", and "How can I afford to make this decision?". For more on this read Robert Kiyosaki's book; *Retire Young, Retire Rich*. You can thank me later.

All of that to say, once you rewire your brain to recognize opportunity you will begin to get hungry for the good ones. I was able to recognize the opportunity present with Northeast so it was easy for me to go for it. Not once did I worry about the amount of money I had to come up with for my initial investment. Instead, my goal was getting my hands on the money to invest so I could realize the full potential of the opportunity.

My decision was not without thought however. I looked at the profit and loss statements. I observed the growth potential. I knew who my partners were. All of these factors combined and pointed to one answer, I had to do this. Failure was never a consideration because the potential for reward far outweighed the risk.

That skill has served me well over and over again. Once you begin to look for opportunity it seems that you find it everywhere. Your attitude changes. You become a better version of yourself. All it takes is the willingness to start. Well that, and you have to actually take action. Here is what I do.

Every year I write out goals for myself. These are not things like "I want to make more money" or "I want to be more successful". No, these are tangible, quantifiable goals. I start by making a list and asking myself a few questions. These might be things like "How much would I like to make this year?", "What other interests would I like to pursue?", "Where am I at physically?", "What do I look like spiritually?", and "Where am I at financially?".

I take this information and compare it against my other goals. I have five and ten year goals. I think of them as brackets. They are broader and bigger than my yearly goals, but they are just as essential to my development as a person. These might be things like "Own a home in such and such place" or "Have x amount in the bank".

My yearly goals should fit into these brackets and should "stack" over time until my fives and tens are realized. The yearly goals tell me how far along I am and whether or not course adjustments need to be made. I might need to come up with something that increases my revenue stream so I can stay on track long term, or I might need to reign in some personal areas to maintain health. Whatever the case, five and ten year goals are a must for me. They do not give me purpose. My purpose comes from another source entirely. However, they do encourage me to live my life "on purpose".

I realize this is something you have probably heard before. There are many self help books and personal development courses on the market that say things similar to what I have mentioned above. It is a record that has been well played.

Here is my secret. I had heard all of that too. I heard it for years and never did anything about it. I also never really did anything as a result. They were nice sentiments, but the action step was lacking and my life showed it in more ways than one. However, when I started to have written goals, things began to change. It is amazing what happens in your life when you have expectations. Normal is considered boring and mediocre just will not do! So stop what you are doing right now and go make some written goals. You will be glad you did.

Another thing I do that has really helped me is I surround myself with people who are bigger than me. People in your life who are more successful than you have a way of pulling you up to their level. They process things differently. Their way of thinking comes from a different perspective. They have already overcome a lot of the challenges you have yet to encounter. They can be phenomenal mentors.

For more on this concept, read a book by Robert Allen and Mark Victor Hansen called *The One Minute Millionaire*. Robert Allen is an entrepreneur who has been around the real estate block a time or two. He is witty, informative, and a great communicator. Mark is most famous for the *Chicken Soup for the Soul* series. He did very well for himself over the years with those books. You might remember seeing them in bookstores unless you lived in a cave.

Yet even with all the success he was frustrated by the earnings wall he kept running into. That changed when he met Tony Robbins at a conference. If you would like to know the rest of the story then go buy the book. It is worth a read (or listen should you get the audiobook). If I were you I would read everything I could get my hands on by these two authors regardless of what your career is. They have an insight and a positivity that is contagious!

Ironically enough, that is the very thing that has really helped me. I read a lot, or I should say I take in a lot of information. It works like this. Doing what I do requires multiple hours on the road. I mean 6 hour one way trips on the road type stuff. Rather than fill my mind with pop music and talk radio, I decided early on to listen to audio books. I took my drive time and turned it into personal development time. I bought scores of audiobooks on the subject of business, leadership, and finance. I would download them to my portable reading device and at times I would even buy an actual book (gasp) and read it in my hotel room at night. This helped keep my perspective sharp and fluid. In the back of this book there is an appendix listing some of my favorite authors and their works. If you like they way I think then you have these individuals to thank for it. I consider them to be kindred souls and mentors to a degree. Purchase their books and read them. You will grow as a professional.

So there you have it. Combine these habits and skills and that is my secret formula for recognizing opportunity. Feel free to try out my methods. You might have a few more that you use or you might try something completely different. The point is you start yourself on a path of personal development that involves shaping your perspective and creating a positive attitude. It may take a few years to develop it on the front side, but the rewards last a lifetime. So I encourage you to do whatever is necessary to make it happen! Train yourself to recognize great opportunities.

CHAPTER 2
SWING BATTER

I love watching my son play baseball. His team won the entire league this past season. They are an impressive bunch of 9 and 10 year olds. Yet they would not be what they are without their team leadership. I have the utmost respect for their coaches. They have to put up with a lot.

If you have never watched a little league game it can be a lot like herding cats at times. The coaches tells them to line up and it looks more like a wad rather than a line. They tell them to swing at the ball. They say this a lot... a whole lot. They scream during the play at the kid holding the ball to throw it to home plate. A lot of times he stands there with a "deer caught in headlights" look on his face. It seems like organization and game mechanics are beyond their reach.

And then it happens. You go to one game and see them work the infield like a major league team. They turn two with the best of them and catch pop flies. When they go to bat they are unstoppable. Runner after runner scores and they end up winning the game in the top of the fourth because of the mercy rule! There is nothing like it.

A great business lesson can be learned in all of this. It is one that we follow at Northeast. A lot of times you will hear the coaches tell (other acceptable words are scream, yell, and shout) at the boys to follow through when they swing. Some of them have a tendency to only swing partially or they do like my son and swing using their wrists. The coach wants them to commit to the swing and follow through. There is a lot of power that gets lost when you "half-swing" at the ball. Batters who follow through send runners flying around the bases. It is a must have skill in order to have a successful team.

It was not long after we purchased Northeast that I realized most people are horrible at just that. They rarely follow through. They have trouble keeping their commitments. This concept is foreign to so many businesses. Landing the account is easy. That is the pre-swing, but you have to commit to the customer to knock it out of the park.

This light switch flipped the first time for me right after we took ownership. I remember it was subtle; hitting me like a cold shower in winter. It seemed like we had no sooner signed all the legal documents to transfer bank accounts and seat ourselves as owners of the business when customers started leaving us in droves. It was horrible.

In fact, we lost half of our existing clientele within the first year. To put that in perspective we served just over three hundred patients when we acquired the business. In two months we were down to one hundred and fifty... ouch!

The bottom line was this. People were unhappy with the service they were receiving and new ownership seemed like a good reason to look for the exit door. They were uncomfortable voicing their concerns to the original owners because they knew them to well. Keep in mind this was a smaller town in Alabama. Everybody knew each other or could make a connection with much less than "Six Degrees of Kevin Bacon" (if you don't know what that is Google it).

There were friendships at stake. However, these people did not know us at all. They did not live in our communities or go to church with us or run into us at the grocery store so leaving at that moment was very easy. It is hard to break a relationship with someone you have known for years. Someone with a face and a name. We were the "outsiders". No name, no face, and no problem for them to leave. That is exactly what they did!

Now I would love to pin blame completely on the former owners, but that would be far too easy and convenient. While I do believe the former owners dropped the ball in certain areas, I am convinced we dropped the ball in just as many areas as well. What happened was more like "A Tale of Two Management Styles". Let me explain.

I have an American bulldog beagle mix named Isabella. She is as cute as can be and loves people. One of the things I noticed after having her for a while was that she would get extremely out of sorts whenever we went for a walk. She was unsure and stressed the entire time. I had owned a few dogs growing up so I was nonplussed.

After doing a little digging (horrible pun I know), it was brought to my attention that dogs need to walk beside you when they are on a leash. Letting them lead the walk is a stressor . They constantly look back for direction and tend to pull the leash holder off in weird directions. It is a wrestling match the entire time. Why? They are not used to setting the course. They need someone to lead! They are not the master therefore tension is created when they feel like they have been placed into that role. This was the very thing that happened to Northeast before we came into the picture.

The former leadership was very reactionary. Everything was a crisis that had to be handled immediately. Our delivery driver would sometimes make three or four trips to the same account to deliver items that were "emergencies", mispacked, or flat out forgotten. This created an environment that was chaotic to say the least. There was no customer service to speak of. There couldn't be, the customers were driving the boat!

As a result they had no confidence in the pharmacy. Most deliveries were late, refill requests were constantly missed, and billing was a complete nightmare. No wonder people were unhappy!

On a side note, you might find the two previous paragraphs to be somewhat strange. Usually you would expect the person in control to feel confident and satisfied, but in business it is the exact opposite. If you let the customer be in control, it wreaks havoc. Your job is to serve the customer, not be controlled by them. If that is occurring in your business you might want to schedule a meeting with your clients and reset expectations. Ok, back to the story.

Enter new owners who are excited about the future and know enough to be dangerous. Grant it, Daniel is a pharmacist and had already successfully established a separate company, but his father Don and myself were totally new to the game; and Northeast Pharmaceuticals was a completely different pharmacy operation than what Daniel was doing at the time. It would be a year before any of us fully understood the animal that was Northeast. In the meantime, we continued to rearrange the furniture on our Titanic and told everybody how nice it looked.

The result was customers were still unhappy, but for different reasons now. We told them things would be different and service would improve, but it did not. We were constantly under the gun to meet delivery deadlines, multiple trips to the same account still occurred daily, and the new employees we hired only added to the chaos. Looking back there are multiple things we would have done differently, but hindsight is always that way is it not? The milk had been spilled so there was no use crying, but we learned one lesson to keep it from happening again.

Here was the common denominator. The problem was not the former owners' "reactionary" management style or the new owners' "aggressive, over compensate" management style. The problem was quite simple and can be summed up as follows... Northeast Pharmaceuticals never did follow through. We never did what we said we would do. We swung the bat, but it was a half-hearted effort.

We would tell people they would have their delivery by 5pm and it might be 7pm due to traffic or a new delivery driver who was not familiar with the area. So? That was not the customer's problem. We told them they would have it by 5pm and they did not. Essentially we lied.

We would also tell customers that we would tweak their bill or credit them for this or that and it may or may not happen. This was because the system we were using was antiquated and credits would not post or worse, they would simply get missed before new statements were printed and mailed. So? That was not the customer's problem either. Again, we were lying to them. It is very easy to see why half of our customers walked away within the first year. The wheels were falling off the bus and we had to put them back on quick!

That January we sat around a conference table in Montgomery, Alabama and discussed the events of the the former year. We posted a loss and had the bruises and low morale to prove it. It was a do or die moment. We considered shutting down. We were on the hook for a few hundred thousand dollars and we were out of reserves. It would be easy to walk away and say we tried. No one would fault us for making a go of it.

It was at that moment that we collectively made a decision. Running would be easy... but that was not an option. That was not our style. Running is for the weak; and we had been through far too much and believed so much in what we were doing that we took it off the table as an option. It was a true burn the ships moment.

So with that decision in place we did something revolutionary... we came up with a plan. Daniel had devised an incentive structure that increased all of our salaries to a point based on sales volume. That helped improve morale. We could feel good about giving ourselves raises if we saw profits increase. So we set sales goals and came up with rewards that we would receive as we achieved each one. We decided to expand our service area and opened our second location in Montgomery. This would serve as a corporate base and an additional pharmacy. That decision could be looked at as somewhat of a premature move since we had no real business in Montgomery, but for us it was another defining moment; another decision to do things better and differently. To understand what that really meant you need to know a thing or two about long term care pharmacy.

For one, it is a very competitive enterprise. My people are out every day calling on competitor's accounts and their people are out calling on my accounts. It is the nature of the business. In order to be successful you need to do one thing really well... be consistent. At the end of the day we always say that anyone can pack medicine in a bottle or blister card. It is how you handle the customer that ensures your success.

With that in mind we looked at the long term care pharmacy model. We took it apart and put it back together again. Most of our competitors were doing everything from a centralized location. That meant they were limited when it came to meeting certain service demands. They suffered in areas such as delivery and order changes. It is hard to switch out a medicine or make a timely delivery when you are geographically centralized and several hours away from many of your accounts.

We took that into consideration and approached the problem a different way. We drew circles on a map of the state of Alabama and decided where we would put pharmacies in those circles to make us easily accessible. We discussed how we would take over the state. Nothing was unattainable. The sky was the limit. Creativity was at an all time high. We had nothing to lose! It was a lot of fun.

In my opinion, that is the second most important decision we made. We decided we were going to excel at customer service. As I said before, anyone can put pills in a bottle or a blister pack and send them out the door. We just wanted to do it better than any of our competitors. That would take a lot of work to accomplish.

Today I can say it STILL takes a lot of work to accomplish, but we do it. This decision to excel at customer service is very easy because of the first important decision we made that set our course for success... do what you say you are going to do. Living out that one phrase has made all the difference.

Recently we had a potential customer ask one of our existing customers what they thought about Northeast Pharmaceuticals. Her response says it all, "They are everything they said they would be". I take pride in our company and our brand when I hear statements like that. If you want to get a leg up on your competition, learn to follow through.

CHAPTER 3
BE HONEST

This chapter is dedicated to the salesperson. They are one of the most crucial parts of any business for without them there would be no growth and ultimately no company to manage. They are the oil and grease that move the machine forward. They make things happen and bring home the bacon.

Being oil and grease they often find themselves in situations foreign to most people. They get caught up in sticky negotiations from time to time. However, a good salesperson doesn't mind getting caught in the gears of negotiation or loosening up the rusty joints of a grumpy account. Their job description involves one thing; getting the customer to "yes".

In order to do that they have to believe in what they are selling. If they have no faith in the product it will show in their sales numbers. They must also have faith in the company. They have to trust the leadership and the boundaries they have been given. If a salesperson is out there tearing it up then you can be assured they believe in your product and have faith in your company. Otherwise they would be working for someone else.

However, there is one other element that is most crucial for their success. One thing has to be trusted more than anything else and confidence in this is an absolute necessity. A great salesperson must trust their instincts. This one thing separates the sheep from the goats.

You see when salespeople trusts their instincts they are like hungry lions on the savannah plains. In a negotiation they know when to give chase; and conversely, when to walk around the deal quietly as if it were a herd of unsuspecting cape buffalo. They have an uncanny intuition. If they played Texas Hold'em they would be dangerous. They do all of this with the precision of a United States military grade Marine ops sniper. Defeat is not in their vocabulary and they do not understand the word "No" (more on this in chapter 8).

As a result, a great boss must trust their sales team. Wait, did I just say that? Yes I did. I think it bears repeating. A great boss must trust their sales team. That can be an incredibly hard thing to do if you are the boss. You are used to calling the shots. You may have built the company from the ground up and think no one knows it better than you.

However, you need to trust your team. Unless you are out there every day you should realize that the people who are out there every day know a thing or two about selling. Let them be oil and grease. Throw them at a deal that is gummed up or a potential account that needs to cook up into something spectacular. That is what oil and grease does best.

There has to be a mutual respect between you and your sales team. If you have that then your company will skyrocket to profitability and greatness. You will be unstoppable. On the other hand if you keep them on a short leash you will have a very small dog to walk. Morale will be low and your bottom line will be lackluster. You have to trust your team! Anyway, all of that was bonus material. Back to the matter at hand.

A salesperson's job description involves getting the customer to "Yes". Getting to "Yes" feels so good. As a result there can be an unreal amount of pressure to make things happen. There can be a tendency to embellish certain aspects of the deal in order to get to "Yes". Couple that with the fact that there is usually a bonus or commission of some sort to be made and you have one very motivated individual on your hands.

And why not? After all, "Yes" feels so good. "Yes" means I get to impress the boss and inflate my ego. "Yes" sets my tone for the week! If you are a salesperson you understand exactly what I am talking about. The temptation to over promise is real and ever present. Fight it at all cost. Instead do one simple very powerful thing. Be honest.

Now there are several reasons to be honest and most of them have nothing to do with morality. Not because I don't believe in morality. I just take that as a given. I think all people want to do the right thing at the end of the day. I really do. I have not met anyone in our organization who wakes up in the morning thinking about ways to swindle Northeast for personal gain.

Even if I suspected that, I would not entertain such ridiculous notions. There is no reason to waste energy on that kind of nonsense. I am too busy trying to find the next deal or establish the next customer relationship. You should be doing the same thing.

You see, the principle is very simple. Without trust nothing works well. I firmly believe we have some of the best, morally good people you will find on the planet working for Northeast. So like I said, my reasons for being honest have nothing to do with morality.

Instead, they have everything to do with being the best. When you have nothing to hide things work so much better. Think about it. When you are honest there are no stories to cover up. Think of the energy that is saved by doing that. Think of the productivity that is gained as a result. When you are honest creativity flourishes. There are no encumbrances or restraints to deal with in an honest environment. This makes us the best choice for our customers. It also makes us the best company for our employees. There are a host of things honesty can do for your organization. Consider the following:

Honesty...

boosts morale.

encourages productivity.

increases efficiency.

builds lasting relationships.

is the best PR.

sells the product.

What a list! Who knew being honest could reap such rewards for your organization. I especially love the last point in the list above. Honesty makes the sale for you. Well it makes the sale for you if you let it. Here is my favorite example to date.

We are asked quite frequently when we do sales presentations if we offer online ordering thru our website. In the world of long term care pharmacy, the ability to go online and reorder a consumer's medicine is a BIG DEAL. Think for a moment with me. You are a nurse and you have 30-50 consumers under your care. All of them take medication and all of them are on at least 3 prescription medicines. Chances are those prescriptions do not run out at the same time. One may run out on the 25th of the month and another medicine might be due for refill on the 28th of the month. If you are a nurse you are responsible for managing this process; and it is a grave offense indeed if you let a consumer miss a dose of medicine.

Enter online ordering. With this tool, nurses do not have to call in refills to the pharmacy. All they have to do is go online, hit a few keys, and submit the order for processing. This saves time, and time equals money for any healthcare facility to operate efficiently.

Long term care pharmacies incorporate this feature into their website at great cost. Most give this access away for free, absorbing the cost of the product in order to gain the business of the healthcare facility. Competition in this area can be pretty cut throat.

So imagine you are one of our sales people and you are asked during a presentation "Do you offer online ordering"? If you are inexperienced there is a temptation present. The temptation is to grasp at straws and mention other products and services that you offer online. You know the type of response... "No, we do not offer online ordering, but we do offer...". That is a mistake.

First, that type of response validates your competition which is something you try to avoid at all cost as a salesperson. Second, it is simply dishonest at its root. You are going to do nothing more than offer your customer a straw man as a solution and they will see right through this.

Instead of these types of responses our sales people are trained to respond honestly. They say something like "No we do not offer online ordering and here is why". That statement does one marvelous thing. It allows our salesperson to tell the story of why we are better and give the customer a solution they may not have considered before. It turns threats into opportunities.

I have never regretted the decision to be honest during a presentation. Sometimes it might mean I do not land an account, but in the long run isn't it better that way? After all, it does no good to land an account by promising them something you can't do, or exaggerating the product. All that does is lead to frustration. That frustration then turns to anger. The anger then leads to a parting of the ways and your name getting thrown around the business community in a manner that is completely unflattering. I would rather not land the account by being honest with what we can't do than land the account and have to pick up the fractured image pieces later. I don't need that kind of PR. It tends to hang around for a while and is hard to over come.

We have garnered a lot of business because of bad salespeople who work for competing pharmacies (notice I said bad salespeople and not bad pharmacies). The reasone is simple. They are commission driven instead of honesty driven. As a result, they land the account by promising the customer all sorts of silly things that they can not do. They promise them the moon and give them a moon rock instead. We don't mind though. All that means is we scoop them up six months or a year later.

So the question still remains, "Why does Northeast Pharmaceuticals not offer online ordering"? Call one of my sales team and ask. I do not want to steal their thunder. They will be more than happy to explain it to you. Include your nursing staff on the call. They will become our biggest fan. As for the rest of you... want to gain customers? Learn to be honest.

CHAPTER 4
LEARN TO NEGOTIATE

There is no greater rush for me than making a deal. I remember reading one of Donald Trump's books where he makes a similar statement. He says at some point in your business the "it" that drives you shifts from making money to doing the deal. At the time I remember thinking "That must be nice!". I also remember thinking that for me the financial component would always be a major part of the equation.

Now I absolutely get it. There does come a point when making money is not the main drive. Being profitable is always fun and exciting, but it eventually takes a back seat to whatever your primary motivation or passion might be. For me, the passion is doing a deal.

Why? Well that is simple. Nothing can ever replace the feeling you get when you walk out of a boardroom with a signed contract. You have landed the plane, gotten the customer to "yes" and it feels great! You are on cloud nine and the world is your oyster.

However, there is much more to it than merely walking in, giving a pitch, and walking away with a signed contract. If that were the case there would never be a bad salesperson! No, it is through the process of negotiation that contracts get signed. In order to get the client to "yes" you have to know how to negotiate. Here are some principles I follow.

First, you must always remember the goal of your negotiation. I think there is a lot of confusion around that point alone. It is tempting to think that the goal of negotiation is to get your client to "yes". However, that is simply a byproduct of a successful negotiation. For me, the primary goal of any negotiation is to craft a deal that exceeds the customer's expectations. I say exceeds because if you craft a deal that meets the customer's expectations any competitor can come along and take that customer away. All they have to do is match your offer, throw in a freebie and poof, your customer will be off to the prom with them instead of you. So I craft a deal that exceeds the customer's expectations. However, this is only possible if I know what their needs are.

In order to do that I must get to know them. The easiest way to do that is let them talk. Now what I am about to say may fly in the face of traditional sales and marketing techniques, but it has worked well for me over the years and I firmly believe in it. Unless you are applying for a job there is no need to walk into a potential client's boardroom and try to impress them with how much you know about their company. It is absolutely unnecessary and robs them of the chance to tell their story. Don't do it. Let them tell their story from their perspective.

Following, is our modus operandi. Typically we begin a pitch describing who we are and what we do. One of us will start with a brief history of the company and then toss the ball to the other partner who will talk about the products and services we offer. At some point near the end of the products and services spill we will say "Now you know a little bit about us, tell us what Such-and-Such place of business does". Then for the next ten minutes we shut up and listen. It is amazing what you learn about a company when you are quiet.

If you are intuitive you will find out all sorts of things about your customer. You will find out their personality type for one. This is a valuable piece of information to have. It is good to know if you will be working with a type A or type B personality.

You will find out why they do their job. Most of the time it is not just a way for them to make money for their families. A lot of people have a mom or dad who worked in the mental health field before them. As a result they followed in their footsteps. I have also met many people that have a loved one or a friend who is mentally ill; they decided to go into mental health to make a difference. Still others were called in to turn the organization around from flailing to flourishing. Whatever the case, I always walk away with a deeper knowledge and a greater appreciation for those who work in the mental health community. It is a true labor of love and these are some of the best people in the world to be associated with. I love to hear their story.

Yet, perhaps the best reason to let them talk is the fact that you will get to find out what their organizational pain is. It may be that they have a budget cut this year and are trying to find ways to fill the revenue hole. They might have a service issue that your company could resolve. Maybe they were hit with a new regulation that you can help them work through or abide by. That is the whole reason you are there after all. They have a pain somewhere and you are trying to alleviate it.

Now please do not misunderstand, you should do your homework and possess a working knowledge of the potential client's company or service. You should know how you can meet their needs before going into a presentation. You should be able to explain why they need to be your customer, but always let them tell their story.

You need to give the customer this chance to shine. They are reminding you why they are important. If it were not for them, you would not be there. Let them take as long as they need to paint an adequate picture of their organization. There will be times during their story that you will want to cut in. You might need clarification on a product or service they offer. You might have questions about their size or scope. Before you know it the conversation moves from a one-sided monologue to a dialogue. You are getting to know the customer. You will not regret this. Let them talk.

Once they are finished the conversation then moves into how we can help them meet their service demands. We discuss things such as residential services, outpatient services, acute care services, assertive community treatment programs, crisis centers and injectable medications as it relates to their nursing staff. A wide net is cast and the negotiation begins.

We tell them what we can do for them and how. A lot of times we are able to overcome setbacks they have had with other pharmacies. These include things such as delivery times, medication errors, and reordering medicine. Once they understand this and want to proceed we schedule a second meeting. I tell them I will email a standard service agreement to them for their perusal.

It is at the second meeting that the rubber meets the road. I love going to those. We discuss things like service terms, concessions, implementation procedures and the like. That is one of my favorite parts. Inevitably we will come to a fork in the road. At that point we will be asked to compromise in an area and we have to be prepared with a response.

The key is knowing HOW and WHAT to compromise. Yes I said how and what. It is a two step process for the art of compromise is just as important as the process of compromise. If you are smart you have built some ready made points of compromise into your service agreement. You have put little things in their that can be wiggled around or completely cut out. If it is an easy negotiation the wiggling and cutting commence, the contract is signed and service begins.

However, sometimes you are asked to compromise on a big item. A potential game changer type thing. It is at this point that you must realize you are standing at the intersection of theory and practice. Keep in mind that the person you are talking with is your customer, not your opponent, and you should be fine. Just shoot straight with them. I can not tell you how many times a potential customer has asked me to concede on a major item and it was nothing more than a smokescreen. This is evident afterward when you hear them say something like "Well you can't fault me for trying now", or some other similar phrase. Yet sometimes they are serious. I have to tell them we can not concede that point, but are willing to make concessions in other areas. All I am doing is shooting straight with the customer. However, I never forget I am trying to craft a deal that exceeds their expectations. Doing this does not require me to give away the farm, but it may require me to sacrifice a sheep or two.

So how do you successfully navigate a negotiation and still turn a profit? The easiest way is to present the customer with several options. We do this is with our packaging. We have four different types that we use. However, there are literally hundreds of variations of these packagings on the market. Some mental health facilities get sold on a particular type of packaging and part of our negotiation involves showing them what types of options we have available. It would be crazy for us to try and stock every type. We would go insane.

Instead, we show the customer the types of packaging we use and allow them to choose the one that best fits their needs. Even though we may not have their preferred option we are still giving them a choice in the matter. This is basic customer psychology 101 and it works! It is like getting your kids to eat vegetables. Instead of telling them they have to eat broccoli you let them choose between eating broccoli or green beans. They may not like either, but somehow giving them a choice in the matter changes things. It gives them a vote and they are more willing to participate in the process.

Here is another example. Remember when your English teacher would give you a writing assignment and the only guideline was "write a three page essay on any topic"? Those types of things drove me nuts growing up. It was as if all of the creativity would drain out of my head and puddle around me on the floor. I would desperately try to think of a topic to write about. The product was always an epic fail. However, when she would say, "Write a three page essay describing either your summer vacation, your dream job, or your favorite hobby", I could write 10 pages because I had a direction to go in! The same concept is at work with our packaging scenario. We are defining the scope for our customer. This allows them to choose the best option for their facility.

Once they decide on an option we move into discussing cycle fills, delivery times, order changes and the like. Again, we let the facility choose what is best for them. If they prefer a morning delivery they get a morning delivery. They get to choose which day of the week to start their medications. They get to choose how much information they want printed on their medication administration record. We give them a lot of choices.

Once that meeting is finished the only thing left to do is run the amended service agreement past the CEO. He irons out any last minute wrinkles, signs it, and they become our customer. Success at last! Negotiation is a beautiful dance. I never get tired of it.

CHAPTER 5
MAINTAINING PERSPECTIVE

Currently I am typing this chapter from 4500 feet. Life looks very different up here. Cars look like bugs moving back and forth across the freeway. Interstates look like small forested paths cutting across the landscape. Farmland and fishponds create this amazing patchwork that looks like a quilt spread out over the countryside. The sky by comparison looks vast and never ending. Today it happens to be the most amazing shade of blue. Every now and then we even pass by a cloud at eye level. You feel like you are in a museum gazing at some priceless work of art. It is very serene.

Well, it is serene until you hear someone squawk through your headphones. Then I realize that it is indeed quite noisy up here after all. I have often watched small aircraft from the ground as they buzz by overhead. They sound like little flies from that vantage point. No real noise to speak of. However, up here in the plane, you have to wear a headset in order to communicate. It is simply too difficult to talk over the prop noise without it.

Also, if you were up here you would notice that there is a constant flurry of activity in the sky that goes virtually unnoticed to those of us who live most of our life on the ground. Pilots chat back and forth with air traffic controllers keeping them abreast of weather conditions, airport regulations, and military exercises. There is constant movement. The pilot switches from one fuel tank to the other to keep the wings balanced. He constantly adjusts the trim. He logs mileage. He adjusts the throttle periodically. He does all of this while the chatter continues in his headset. I get to hear all of this through the pair of cans strapped to my head. It feels like I am 8 years old again eavesdropping on one of my parent's private conversations.

Finally, I almost forgot about this, there are things inside the aircraft itself that most people never get to see. Take the instrument panel for example. You never get to see this side of air travel when you fly commercially, but in a small aircraft there are all sorts of instruments on the dashboard. They measure everything from oil pressure to altitude and are scattered from one side of the plane to the other. They light up, blink, and spin. It looks impressively complicated. I am glad I am not responsible for getting us to our destination. We would never make it! Instead Roger, the aircraft pilot, will be handling this task. He is a seasoned pro and has never failed me yet.

So what is the point of this little foray into the wonderful world of flight? In a word it is PERSPECTIVE. There is a tendency to think that our little world is the only world that exists. The truth of the matter is just that... our world is little. Huge problems are indeed huge in a little world. They are not so menacing when you can zoom out though. It does me good to be reminded that my little world is a part of the whole when it comes to business. In fact, we all need to be reminded of this at times. Just like flying, perspective allows me to zoom out and see the big picture as it pertains to Northeast. This accomplishes several things.

First, it allows me to make good decisions about problems within the company. I need perspective to handle employee complaints, wage increases, productivity obligations, and scheduling. It has often been said that the devil is in the details and this is very true when it comes to managing employees. Lose perspective and there is a tendency to pick favorites, punish and reward unjustly, or turn into a taskmaster.

Perspective reminds me that our employees, though they work for me, are ultimately employed to achieve the goals and objectives set out for Northeast Pharmaceuticals. As a result, my emotions and bias can be somewhat removed from the picture. I am less likely to make snap decisions or unwarranted judgment calls that might damage morale or worse, the company. Managing employees becomes much easier and efficient when the proper perspective is maintained.

Perspective is also a great thing to have when it comes to customer relations. Every business owner has that one account that is very demanding and oftentimes resorts to threats in order to get their way. These threats come in various forms. The two I most frequently hear are "It would be a shame if we had to take our business somewhere else because of this matter", or "If you can not do such and such we will have no other option but to look elsewhere for pharmacy services".

Perspective allows me to see which accounts have valid concerns, some are always unhappy no matter what you do; and also helps me see if losing that account will adversely affect the company. Some of you know exactly what I am talking about. There are certain customers that always have an issue with something. No matter how large the perceived problem they usually just need someone to listen to them for a bit and all is right with the world. Perspective helps me see that.

Other threats have much more validity. You know those types too. When the phone rings on your end those are the calls you do not miss. Something is wrong in Camelot and ignoring the problem simply will not do. You have to get involved. You have to take action. The threat is real.

Again, it is impossible to do that if you lack the proper perspective. I have picked up several accounts because our competitors lacked the proper perspective when it came to customer service. Where they did not take issues seriously, we did. As a result, we gained business.

Here is another advantage of maintaining perspective. This is one you might not have thought of. Perspective helps you thin the herd at times. At Northeast, if an account generates little revenue, makes multiple veiled threats, and is a drain on company resources... they might be a good candidate to be some other pharmacy's client.

I know in the beginning we had several accounts that were an absolute drain on us as a company. They generated minimal amounts of revenue. They had our delivery drivers burning up the road with multiple daily trips due to so called "emergencies". They were some of the grumpiest people you would ever want to meet. I mean just flat out miserable. When we lost them at first we thought it was the end of the world. Losing business always puts you in fear of the domino effect. However, our perspective was still cloudy since we had only purchased the business four months previously. Knowing what we know now we would have thrown a party! Oh the things experience can teach you. It can certainly help you do some "client pruning" should that time ever come.

Maintaining proper perspective makes it a lot easier to deal with both of the issues mentioned above, however there is one thing perspective does that is vital. It keeps me from making major mistakes. That alone makes it a valuable practice to perfect. Take to heart the following example.

Our pharmacy sends out thousands of customer bills each month. it is a necessary evil. I am also pleased to report that our AR department runs a monthly collection percentage of 96%. Our team performs phenomenally well. Yet there are always those extenuating circumstances where an organization owes us money for several months. The temptation is to call in the note immediately. However, it is imperative to keep a proper perspective of the situation or you risk losing the customer. We lost one a few years back because we lacked the proper perspective. Here is the story.

We had been servicing this particular mental health facility for a couple of years. They had expansion plans and we were excited. In fact, they had already expanded their operation by about 30 or so clients since coming on board with us. Things were going great as far as we knew. We even opened another pharmacy that was closer to them and began servicing their facilities out of this new location.

Then it happened. There were service issues. Our new pharmacy was not prepared to handle the account because they had been poorly trained. The staff were brand new and everything went nuts. Deliveries were not arriving on time, meds were packaged incorrectly, and some orders were flat out missed. Needless to say we got a phone call for a meeting to resolve the issues.

Keep in mind that this account generated about $40,000 worth of revenue per month. That's right, $40,000. In the meeting the service issues were discussed and the customer asked us to move their service location from our new pharmacy back to the pharmacy in Montgomery. We shot that idea down because logistically it made no sense. They were reluctantly ok with that; and then the proverbial fertilizer hit the fan. Some of the patients at that facility owed us money and had owed us money for months. We did not handle the collection process properly during the meeting. A few misguided statements were made and that sunk our ship. They were already disgruntled because we refused to service them out of Montgomery, so we ended up losing the account.

I called our corporate office and was not happy to say the least. I had landed that account two years previously after a six month negotiation and wanted to know what happened! When I asked about the money they owed I was told that they owed us several thousand dollars and one location had not paid us in 6 months! Sounds horrible right? I called our billing department. As it turned out, the location that had not paid us for 6 months owed a whopping $250.

Now the facility as a whole did have a balance prior to that of several thousand dollars, but we structure our contracts in such a way that the facility is not responsible for payment. The consumer's at the facility own their own debt. The facility should have NEVER received a call from us asking about money, but they did. And to their credit, the facility was always good about helping collect that money from the consumer's if we notified them in a timely manner.

All I was told was that they owed us money and one location had not paid us for 6 months! We lost that account over $250 and an out of line attitude. I know this because I spoke with the executive director about the matter personally. I also know this because one of my colleagues ran into her husband at an unrelated event. He did not mention the money, but he made a point to mention the attitude problem. I was not present at the meeting by design, yet I made every effort to mend the fence. However, it was too little too late.

So you might be wondering how that has played out between me and the executive director. Do we dodge each other at conferences? Is there an awkwardness when we meet? Nope, on the contrary, she and I are on a first name basis today. What she did was make a business decision. Neither one of us took it personally. I have the utmost respect for her and her team. They do on incredible job. I would love to have their business back, have another chance, etc; but I do not blame them one bit for their decision. If it had been me I would have done exactly the same. We lost perspective. We blew it.

CHAPTER 6
FEELING CONFLICTED?

At some point in your business things are going to blow up for one reason or another and you are going to have to deal with conflict. It is not easy, but handling these situations is absolutely necessary in order for things to run smoothly. If you do not manage conflict well, it will own you at the end of the day.

Before we dive into the basic principles of handling conflict I think there is one vital element that makes or breaks conflict resolution... You. That's right, you are the hinge in the whole affair and people will be looking to you to see how effectively the hinge operates. If the hinge is ineffective all sorts of problems could arise. So with that stated, I would like to put the mirror in front of your face as a leader and give some opportunity for self-critique. Following are a few different types of leadership portraits that could easily spell disaster. If your leadership style resembles one of these you might want to consider retooling a bit before you have to handle your next company issue or employee problem.

The Heavy Handed Leader

You know this type of leader. They have a short fuse and the blood pressure to prove it. Their motto always seems to be "Use a bigger Hammer". Listening skills are in short supply with this individual and you better run, duck, or cover if you get on their bad side. If this describes your leadership style I would like to remind you of a few things.

If you are too heavy handed no one in your organization will want to bring their problems to you. You will be viewed as someone who is too volatile to deal with; who's reasoning is inconsistent and hard to follow. The way your employees will deal with this is simple... they will avoid you at all cost. Last time I checked avoiding leadership when making decisions is a bad thing. You need to be in the loop as the leader. You must realize you take yourself out of that loop when you deal with conflict in a heavy handed manner.

The end result is your company could wither and dry up. Employees will seek employment elsewhere. Customers will find another company to do business with if their cares or concerns are always met with hostility. If your turnover rate is high or your sales are eroding, chances are you are being too heavy handed as a leader.

The Indecisive Leader

This same principle is also at work on the other side of the coin. Some leaders have a hard time making decisions. They constantly waffle between getting this person's opinion or seeking "legal" advice. They will consult with everyone at every level before they make a decision... pardon me, if they make a decision. The fact that a decision has to be made about a particular conflict is too much for them to handle so they end up talking with everyone ABOUT the problem, but never truly HANDLE the problem. If this looks familiar to you, take a look at what could happen to your business below.

If you are afraid to make a decision because of HR concerns, employee lawsuits, customer relations, or other reasons, your company will implode. People will put up with a lot, but they do not respect lack of action. "No action" is always perceived as weakness on the part of the leader from an employee standpoint.

Once this perception of you is out there, it is a very hard thing to overcome. Employees will not stick around for weak leadership because they know that no one has their best interest in mind at the end of the day. Let that marinate for a minute. Your employees are expecting you to have their best interest in mind at all times, especially when it comes to handling conflict. Therefore, it is perfectly ok to make a decision and act on it! Even if they do not agree with your decision they will respect you tremendously for taking action.

Customers, however, will do just the opposite. They can turn into bullies if you do not take action and address their concerns. You will find yourself bending over backwards to accommodate their needs because you failed to handle the conflict. This is a drain on your staff and your bottom line. Over time the same thing happens in this scenario as it does with the heavy handed leader. Employees will leave and customers will run away. So we come to the same conclusion. If your turnover rate is high or your sales are eroding, it might be time for you to make a few decisions!

The Tunnel Vision Leader

This last type is particularly intriguing. Some leaders have tunnel vision and lead with it. These types tend to believe the first story presented to them is gospel truth and act accordingly without giving ear to the other side. They are willing to take up the first cause or injustice they see and act swiftly to administer punishment and correct the situation. The only problem is there is always another side. Take the following example from my childhood.

I remember one time my brother got in trouble for something. We were about 9 or 10 yrs old then and were typical boys; always taking things apart to see how they worked. VCR's, radios, toasters... if it had a plug and was held together with screws, we were getting inside to see what made it tick. When our curiosity was satisfied and we knew what made it tick, we would put it back together. There was usually no tick after that. In fact, what followed was a period of silence. The silence was then followed by a feeling of overwhelming dread and stomach knotting terror! You have to understand, my mother had told us repeatedly NOT to take things apart but we did anyway; or I should say, I did anyway. I was usually the culprit (ok, replace usually with always).

Anyway, back to the story. I remember thinking at the time that I did not know why he was getting in trouble because I had not seen him take apart anything. Yet, I sat in silence in my bedroom and listened to him cry as he was getting a spanking. I was feeling quite accomplished with myself and somewhat scott free when it happened. It was as if my world blurred momentarily and began to move in slow motion. I heard my brother say in a staccato, stammering, cry five words that changed my destiny... "But mom, Jason did it!". I don't think I need to tell you what happened to me after that. My rear end is still smarting.

You may have a similar story from your childhood. If you do, you may recall how it felt to get punished for something you did not do. You fell victim to tunnel vision leadership. Swift judgment was made based on incomplete information. Tunnel vision leaders tend to do that a lot. They hear one side, process it quickly and go take immediate action without giving ear to the other party('s) story. If this picture looks like you then consider what can happen as a result of your snap leadership decisions.

You will be manipulated plain and simple. Employees will capitalize on the fact that you tend to believe the "first version" of a story. If it seems like you are constantly handling a stream of conflict check yourself to see if you are being too gullible. The last thing you need is a complaint line starting at your door. It will drain your energy and leave you mentally exhausted. Your working environment will resemble a classic western movie. Whoever shoots first wins! You don't want that.

Also, your customer base will exhaust you. You will begin to look at them as leeches while totally blind to the fact that you let it happen! People only manipulate if you let them. The customer may be unhappy for a reason, but there is also another perspective that is just as valid. The best way to navigate this is to give ear to BOTH sides before making any decision. I would even add, give ear to both sides before making a decision no matter how long it takes! Failure to do so brings us back to the same place... high turnover and eroding sales. If the above scenarios describe you, it might be time for you as the leader to open both eyes!

Now I can not help the way you are wired up. Some people innately try to avoid conflict. They would rather jam slushee straws in their eyes than deal with a problem. Others seem to thrive off of it. You can literally see their face break into a smile at the thought of going toe to toe with someone over an issue. Everyone has a personality and you know which type you are. It is good to keep this in mind as you approach conflict. You do not want to become a part of the problem, you are there to solve it.

Here are some principles I try to use and you may be surprised at where they come from. There is a little known book called the Bible that has some really great and useful information in it. I pull my conflict resolution from Matthew Chapter 18. It reads as follows:

"If your brother or sister sins, go and point out their fault, just between the two of you. If they listen to you, you have won them over. But if they will not listen, take one or two others along, so that 'every matter may be established by the testimony of two or three witnesses'. If they still refuse to listen, tell it to the church; and if they refuse to listen even to the church, treat them as you would a pagan or a tax collector.

Matthew 18:15-17

It works every time. Now you may have never read the Bible or you might follow a religion that has another holy book with similar principles you practice. I am not discounting your approach, I am telling you what works for me. Based on that passage above, here are the principles I use.

1. Always go to the offending party(ies) first. It is very easy to ask everyone around you about a situation and couch it in terms like "I am just getting clarity", or some other nonsense phrase. The bottom line is you are engaging in gossip and that will poison your organization. Sit down with the person(s) directly. It is the best way to get to the root of the issue. It is also the right thing to do.

2. Each side has validity. To revisit the Tunnel Vision Leader for a moment, we tend to believe people in our world who are closest to us. Always keep this in mind when your are dealing in business matters. You are biased towards those people you work closest with on a daily basis. When they come to you with a concern there is immediate validity because of your relationship with them. You owe it to the other side to hear their version of the truth. That perspective is just as valid.

3. Once a decision has been made, it has been made. Another way of saying this is there is no need to rehash a scenario or beat a dead horse after the fact. If that continues you have grounds for termination if it is an employee. If it is a customer you might consider releasing them and letting them be a "blessing" to one of your competitors. Decisions, especially ones that involve conflict, should have an air of finality to them. We are moving forward, no need to go back and reopen a wound.

So there you have it. Wouldn't it be nice to go about our routine, focus on customer service, and never have to deal with conflict? Yeah I think that would be amazing! However, that is never going to be the case when running a business. Conflict resolution is going to be a necessary part of what you do as a leader.

Did you hear that? It is going to be a necessary part of what you do. That means no way around it, no easy outs, no free passes, no mulligans! This is a have to, not a maybe. All you have to do is one thing. Handle the conflict well. That means being consistent and definitive with your decisions. The payoff should be obvious at this point. Learn to handle conflict and you gain respect from your employees. They will go to the ends of the earth for you. Your business will thrive!

CHAPTER 7
GENERATING SALES

One of the most challenging aspects of running our pharmacy was discovered early on. You may not realize this, but in order for you to turn a profit you must land a sale every so often. My business partner and close friend Don Mims says it this way, "Sales cover a multitude of sins". That could not be a more true statement.

When sales are flowing, revenue dips and cash flow anomalies are easy to deal with. I mean who cares if you overspent by $2,000 in marketing if you generated an extra $30,000 that month in sales. It is easy to cover up. However, let four or six months go by without a single sale and you will be singing an entirely different song. I know this because it has happened. Rather I should say it happens. That is the reality of selling. It is cyclical. You go for months and months appearing to be unstoppable. Then you enter a sales drought and the entire world seems to cave in.

What's the answer to this dilemma? Quite simple. Learn to generate sales. Once you are able to do this you will discover that droughts are predictable. They are less scary and even somewhat necessary to the process. You will also generate more business than you know what to do with. Several different methods have worked for us.

One of my personal favorites is mining existing customers for leads. In fact, that is how we achieved momentum in the beginning. It all started with West Alabama Mental Health Center.

We had been in business for about a year when we stumbled into our niche market of mental health. I remember it clearly. Daniel sent me an email with potential leads. I took one look at it and thought, "This is not our clientele at all. We service assisted living facilities and community service homes. This is a list of substance abuse programs". I sent a reply asking if he thought these leads were worth our time. His response was that he did not know. He came across them on the internet and forwarded them to me on a whim; but he thought going through them would not hurt anything either.

So I did. I went down the list and systematically knocked off each one. They were odd things like a day program, a state bid, or a private pay residential facility. I know many of you reading this book just went "Huh"? All you need to know is these were not the types of places we serviced. They were not a good fit for the types of things we offered. So I was thinking again that this was just another dead end list from the internet.

Then I came across something I was unfamiliar with. There was a listing for a West Alabama Mental Health Center. I could not get a clear picture of who they were or what they did so I called them and scheduled a meeting with the executive director and her clinical staff. The meeting went great! We could really help this place. Medication administration was taking up too much of their time. Our system could help them reclaim hours, maintain efficiency, and decrease the potential for error! Within two weeks I received a call back and we started servicing our first mental health center.

It was a beautiful marriage. They loved what we were able to do, or I should say they love what we are able to do because they are still with us today. I am grateful for their support and glad they gave us a chance. However, they also did something else for us that really put us on the map. They gave us a lead.

Three months into servicing them we scheduled a call back meeting to make sure our team was meeting their expectations. In that meeting, we asked them one simple question that you should always ask if you are doing a good job with your customers. We said, "Is there anybody else you know who might benefit from our services"? That reply led us to Southwest Alabama Mental Health, which led us to Baldwin County Mental Health, which eventually led us to just under half the mental health centers in the state! That's right, our saturation of the Alabama mental health market can be traced back to one question. That is remarkable indeed!

Now, I can already hear some naysayers reading this who might be thinking that I am oversimplifying the whole affair. "Surely there was more to it than that", you might hear them say.

Ok, here is round two. This one involves my friend Jason Ragsdale. At the time, he and his wife Stephanie ran the Baptist Children's Group Home near Dothan, Alabama. He and I were childhood friends and had recently been reconnected through his cousin Trey who is also one of my childhood friends.

We started servicing Jason because of my friendship with him. I will never forget the first batch of medicine I delivered to his group home. It was a whopping 5 prescriptions. You read that right, 5 prescriptions. I drove two hours from Montgomery to Dothan to deliver five prescription medications. The other side of the story is that we knew this going in. He told us his home would not be a huge money maker, and my reply was I was happy to service him anyway. We wanted to make things easier for him and his staff. We would deliver the medicine saving them a trip to the local retail chain pharmacy. This gave them more time to interact with the kids in the home. That is always a good thing.

Anyway, we did the same thing with him. After a few months of service we asked if he knew of any other group homes that might benefit from what we do. He thought for a minute and mentioned a girl's home about three miles down the road from his. We scheduled a meeting, began servicing them, and two weeks later asked them the same question.

That reply led to one of our largest accounts in Dothan. All of that from 5 prescriptions and two questions, wow!

The simple truth in these two examples is that your customers are one of the most valuable sources for lead generation. Use that to grow your business. If you are taking care of them, ask the right follow up questions and you will be amazed at what you discover. Most often, they will have no problem throwing business your way and that is one of the highest compliments you can receive!

Another method of generating sales are the conferences we participate in throughout the year. You may have to do some digging, but chances are you can find some trade shows in your area to participate in. We attend a few shows religiously. We set up a table armed with product samples and giveaways. The rest is self explanatory. Patrons attending the conference are given free time that they can use to explore the exhibit hall. As they pass through we share with them a picture of what we do.

Now I know some of you might have groaned when you heard the word "trade show" or "conference". You might think that they are a complete waste of time or a drudgery at best. You spend hours sitting behind an exhibit table waiting on fifteen or thirty minutes of golden time when potential customers herd through like cattle. They grab your pens, candy, and anything else that is not tied to the table! You can't wait for the last day of the conference hoping you can pack up and leave early if it is dead. I realize I just lost some of my readership for a paragraph, but the rest of you are bent double laughing.

I know they can be boring at times, but you should never underestimate the networking potential of a good conference. I remember the first year we attended the conference put on by the Alabama Council of Community Mental Health Boards in Birmingham. We were brand new to the game and went with the intent of getting to know people. The entire affair was orchestrated by Jim and Diane Dill who are the executive directors of the ACCMHB. They reached out to us with an invite and we were more than happy to attend and make some connections.

Keep in mind we had never done anything like this before. Our competitors show up with huge displays, impressive pamphlets, and incredible giveaways. Their booths looked like great circus tents. They were eye catching and engaging. A few even had interactive videos with product demonstrations and the like. We showed up with examples of our packaging, some pens, business cards, a banner to hang behind our booth, and two legal pads. By all accounts our booth looked pitiful.

Don and I looked at each other and laughed after we set up. Others had gotten there the night before and spent an hour or so getting ready. I think we took a whopping ten minutes. We spread out our packaging and information cards and were ready to go. Other competitors cast a condescending gaze at us as they walked by our booth in their high heels and power suits. We had been minimized and discounted because of our paltry little display.

However, there are two things you need to realize about Don Mims and Jason Britt. We are very good at what we do. In fact, we are the best. We love engaging people and explaining our business to potential customers; and that is exactly what we did at the conference. Armed with a clipboard and ambition, we made connections and set appointments for the next two days.

It was comical to watch our competitors (who we did not really know at the time) try to woo customers with nice displays and pretty employees. Our approach was totally different. While everyone else was busy giving away $50 gift cards, we were busy getting to know people; we were asking them who we should talk to about what Northeast could do for their organization.

Now do not misunderstand, we give away $50 gift cards every year now. It is a way to support the conference and hype up the crowd with a drawing. In fact this year, we were the premier sponsor for the conference. Jim and Diane gave us a shot in more ways than one with that initial invite. They were also instrumental in helping me make connections in other states. It is our pleasure to support their work. They are the best and there is none better as far as I am concerned.

However, the point of the conference from my perspective as a business owner is to make connections. That can sometimes get lost in translation when you are an employee. It is good to remind yourself why you are really there. I'm not there to make friends with other vendors, or make my booth better than the competition's, or have the best giveaway. I may accomplish all of those things, but that is not why I am really there.

They should not be your reason either. No one has ever agreed to an appointment with me because they found my exhibit booth to be alluring and engaging. They do business with me because I took time to make a connection. Work your conference the right way. We took two legal pads and did quite alright the first year!

The last method we have used to generate sales is simple. We give our employees an incentive. Every employee gets rewarded for good leads that turn into bankable customers. We reward them for "hunting the bird" for us. The way this works is as follows. We pay anyone in our company a one time bonus of $10 per patient for any lead they generate that turns into a Northeast customer. That bonus is paid the month following revenue generation.

For example, let's say one of our employees gives us a lead on a one hundred bed facility in March. We land the account in July and are able to realize revenue in August. They are paid a $1,000 bonus in August. Very simple, yet very effective. For us it makes perfect sense.

You have to understand, covering several states now is an enormous task. Even with three owners, trying to balance effective management and grow the bottom line is challenging. Add to that the front loading process of mining new states for potential leads and it could be three months before we have anything solid. By offering incentive, the employees who live in these states are my eyes and ears. Lead generation is much quicker and more efficient since they are already familiar with the area! The end result is we gain traction and momentum quicker in new territories. This means more sales, and more sales means a nice long future for Northeast.

CHAPTER 8
NO NEVER MEANS NO

One of the best residential facilities for mental retardation and the mentally ill is in a small town near Montgomery, Alabama. It is our pleasure to serve them. They have an attention to detail and a level of care that makes you proud. We often use them as a model for practice, or a reference when we are giving a pitch. The way we got their business was two-fold at the time.

They had been using an out of town pharmacy for their needs and it simply was not working. For one, the packaging method was not a good fit. We had more options and were a lot closer. I remember them saying that no one from that pharmacy had ever visited them. With us as their pharmacy, they receive daily contact via our delivery driver (previously their meds had been shipped via a 3rd party courier). They also have an individual that is assigned to their account, access to a person in our sales department... and they can always call me or Don if they need anything. Those things were a big selling point for them.

The other selling point was a common one... billing. They were holding a $46,000 bill in their hand and wanted to know if we could help with that. Now, we could not help what they owed their pharmacy, but with us we did promise their experience to be different. Billing is one of those enigmas that can either make or break you as a pharmacy. You have to deal with a lot of 3rd party providers, and they all have different prescription drug coverage plans. Certain items can be billed out and certain items can only be billed for certain quantities. There are coverage gaps to contend with, non-covered items and the like. You name it; the list is endless. We made sure early on that we had the right people in charge of our billing department.

Long story short, we got there business and we have yet to give them a $46,000 bill. Now that is not to say that we have not had to work through our relationship at times. Things can get kinked here and there with process, delivery, and yes... billing. The difference between us and their old pharmacy is we are willing to sit down and make it work. We will fix problems. We will try something new if they want to do something different. Relationships take work and our relationship with them is living proof that hard work pays off.

However, in the beginning they said "No". Rather the owner said "No". We wanted the whole ball of wax, but she was unwilling to give it away and for good reason. Here is how it played out.

It was a picture perfect sunny afternoon when Don and I found ourselves in downtown Prattville looking for this particular facility. We had driven around a neighborhood for about 15 minutes looking with no luck. Exasperated we stopped to ask a lady for directions. She was sitting on her front porch enjoying the day. I rolled down the window and asked if she knew where the facility was located. Her response was priceless. She causally pointed across the street and said "Right there!". We had driven past it no less then 5 times.

We turned into the parking lot and went inside to find out who we needed to meet with. Once inside, we discovered that the person we needed to talk to was not there. So we scheduled a meeting, came back, did the pitch, and she gave us a shot. As it turned out, she had two locations, Prattville and Troy. We developed a plan to phase in the Prattville location. Then Don asked when we could begin servicing the residential center in Troy and we were met with a nice big "No".

She was unwilling to make any changes to the location in Troy because everything was going well. We are always huge fans of "If it is not broken don't fix it", so we understood her reasoning. Plus, we were a new relationship so it made sense to test the waters for a while. Fast forward two years and we are servicing the Troy location as well. What was the difference? In a word it was timing. I can not explain it other than to say it was just simply not the right time for us to service that location. However, had we taken "No" as our final answer we would still not be servicing that location. We were always reminding them that we would love to have all of their business. All we had to do was wait. Lesson learned... No never means no.

You should right that down, tattoo it on your arm, and repeat it every morning. No never means no. It simply means not right now. If we took every "No" at face value we would not have half of the business that we currently possess. The trick is understanding the psychology of "No".

People say "No" for different reasons. You should never take "No" personally. You should still believe you are the best option around. Then, you should learn to manage the "No". Follow up with the potential customer every few months. Let them "know" that you are not afraid of their "No". Tell them you would love to have their business and are free at any time to come back and show them all of the services your company has to offer. Over time, if you are solid, you will probably get them to "Yes". When that occurs it is a great feeling!

Here are a few reasons "No" has turned into "Yes" for us :

- Staffing changes with the potential account
- The pharmacy they were using went out of business
- New state regulations
- Expansion
- Fee increases
- Word of mouth from a colleague who is one of our customers
- Safety concerns

- Timing
- Persistence

The bottom line is "No" is a temporary word. It should not scare you. When you believe in what you have to offer, "No" tends to become nothing more than a formality. I can not tell you how many times I have heard "We are happy with our current provider and have no intentions of changing". I always find that really funny when I am sitting in an exec's office. If they are happy, why am I there? They are simply fencing me in so they can observe what we have to offer and make an educated decision from there. I am ok with that. Again, the key is you have to learn to manage the "No". It can mean many things, but one thing is certain, it never means No!

CHAPTER 9
IF IT WERE EASY...

Four years into our adventure we were starting to saturate the Alabama market and looking to move into other states. Our service specialty was residential mental health group homes and we serviced just under half of the total number of group homes in the state. From time to time someone would ask what we offered in the way of outpatient services and our response was that we did not service outpatients.

Mental health outpatient clinics operate just like your regular doctor's visit. You see him or her, they administer a diagnosis, give you a prescription, and you are out the door. You can choose any pharmacy you want to fill your prescriptions. Because of this, there is no guarantee that mental health patients will choose to do business with us.

So for years we opted not to tap this market for business. However, everywhere we went people kept asking us what we would do for their outpatient programs. It became too much to ignore so we began to explore the opportunity. We took a look at what our competitors were doing in this area which was not much at all. We looked at a few different service models. We unpacked those models and put them back together again. Then it happened.

We were exploring a brand new state, Mississippi. When I say exploring I mean we were at a conference in Philadelphia, MS exhibiting as a vendor (remember that chapter on generating sales?). We were making new connections. As it turned out we discovered there was another conference in two months that was exclusive to mental health. So we registered and went to that one in October.

It was there that we were introduced to Life Help Mental Health, based in Greenwood, MS. They were interested in what we had to offer so we scheduled a meeting and made the six hour; yes... six hour, drive from Montgomery, Alabama. Turns out they had a solid, established relationship with a local pharmacy. Unwilling to compromise that relationship, the conversation turned to outpatient services. We picked their brain, talked about different service methods, and left there promising to give them a proposal for what we would do.

Back at the office I put something together and let my business partner Daniel eyeball it. It was a very basic proposal. All it said in a nutshell was "Hey, we would like a shot at servicing these people. Here is how we plan to do that". I think the entire proposal was less than 6 pages. There were some clauses in there about possibly putting a pharmacy on site, a mention of providing residential services in the future, but the main thrust of the proposal centered around us servicing the outpatient population.

They agreed and we started. It was a totally new market for us. We had never done anything like this before. They were going to be the guinea pig, they just did not know it. We never wanted them to find out. In order to do that we made a commitment amongst ourselves to pay special attention to them from day one.

We developed a plan to phase in all of the clinics and stuck to it. It went swimmingly well. We could not believe it. The numbers were there, the bottom line was swelling, and the people genuinely liked what we had to offer. We were on to something and that something was good!

Fast forward a few months and we now have an operation that services two other large mental health facilities in that state. We pursued the same strategy, and implemented the same plan. We assumed we would get the same revenue results.

However, the results were less than dazzling. It seemed that Life Help was the exception, not the rule. Now I am not saying that the other accounts are not profitable, but their yield is not proportionate to what we experienced in Greenwood. We were starting to do the same thing in Alabama and it was becoming clear that this was going to be work.

We were ok with the work, but we were not prepared for some of the things that were going to happen. As it turned out, Mississippi Medicaid threw everyone a curve ball. They made a decision to have only two main providers for the state. They sent a letter to everyone notifying them of the change. However there is one problem with sending a mentally ill person a letter notifying them of changes to their prescription drug plan. You guessed it, they are mentally ill. They do not have the capacity to understand or process the information, and that is assuming they even read the letter!

We received a letter too... one week before the switch. The switch was to occur January 1st of the next year and we received a letter notifying us of the change the week after Christmas. We had no time to be proactive. The mental health center never received a letter at all. In short, what followed was a nightmare.

Our pharmacies tried to process claims on January 1st for meds that were billable 4 weeks earlier only to get rejection notices. Essentially this meant that we could not send out medicine for those consumers because their "new" plan would not pay for it. We called Life Help to see what was going on. Between the two of us we got it worked out.

The consumers were upset. They had to write a letter stating that they wanted to stay with their current prescription drug plan. The letter they received in the mail stated that if they did not pick a new plan one would be chosen for them by default. So on January first, scores of our customers had a new prescription drug plan that would not pay for medicine they had been taking for years. They did not understand what had happened and since we were their pharmacy it was our fault. They left in droves and it was hard to get them back. In fact, we are still trying to get some of them back. We were so mad at the situation we could spit nails, but what good would that do?

There are times in life when you have epiphanies and I am going to give you one right now. If any part of your business involves dealing with the federal government as a payer source be prepared for severe frustration. They are the worst managers on the planet; and are constantly seeking ways to take money out of the states hands and place it under federal control. This creates more hoops to jump through, more paperwork to fill out, and more chaos in the long run.

For example, in some cases where they are our primary payer source they have stretched out payment terms from 30 days to 45 days. This creates quite a challenging revenue gap to fill. In other cases they have not honored our contracted rate. They never come back to us and say "We recently discovered that we told you we would pay 'x' amount. Our records indicate that we shorted you by 'x' amount. Let us make it up to you". No it is up to us to go behind them and make sure they are paying us correctly. The mantra of any government payer source seems to be "prove it"!

So why am I telling you all of this? Simple. Some things are going to be beyond your control. You can whine about it all day long, but it will do no good. We know the government is going to be inefficient at anything they attempt to do. This is a known variable. Ranting and raving about it does you no good. It drains you mentally and is totally unproductive. You could spend that time doing a million other things. Develop a plan to deal with it and understand that you are constantly going to have to adapt your plan.

That one word is key. Adaptation. It is the name of the game. You are going to have to clean up someone else's mess from time to time in order to conduct business. In that one example, we had to jump over hurdles with Medicaid and Medicare, apologize for situations we did not create, and fight to keep our customers! All because a decision was made by the government to streamline their process. I think they had a good idea, but they were horrible with the execution.

And those are not the only hurdles we have had to overcome. We have had to deal with local pharmacy's threatening to sue us because we are "taking business" from them. Last time I checked there was no stamp on any of us that says "I belong to such and such pharmacy". They have just gotten used to sitting behind a counter and waiting on business to come to them. We are forward thinking and proactive. We go after it.

Other challenges involve angry consumers. They can get downright mad when they misunderstand the process. They usually call the mental health facility and end up chewing on the receptionist. That person can end up hating us if we don't intervene.

Beyond that there are doctors to deal with. Some like what we offer, others do not. Some work with us to make sure the process of the patient receiving their medicine is efficient, others write a script and dare you to ask them to do anything more because they are after all, a "doctor".

Throw in HIPPA compliance, narcotic regulations and restrictions regarding prescription medicine and all of a sudden this wonderful new market looks like a monster! There is a temptation to run for the door. The heat can get turned up at times and it is no fun when you realize you are the frog in the pot!

To all of that I have one response. Daniel and Don say this all the time and it has become somewhat of a mantra for us as a company... "If it were easy, everyone would be doing it". Now I am sure this is not the first time you have heard that phrase or something like it. I just think it does good as a leader to remind yourself of that basic principle.

If you are running a business, leading people, maybe starting a new project from scratch, or in the beginning stages of birthing a new idea; remember that statement. If it were easy, everyone would be doing it. It sounds so rudimentary because it is. I will say it again. If it were easy everyone would be doing it.

Since it is not easy, YOU are doing it. If you believe what you are doing is worthwhile you will find a way to make it happen. At work we have three ways to make ideas happen. Their names are Daniel, Don, and Jason. We are formidable when it comes to business acumen. We are also used to "not easy". In fact, it is almost an expectation. We have adopted the attitude that "anything that is worthwhile, is typically not easy". You will find the same to be true in your business and leadership. The really neat part though is this; if you press on you will realize your reward. That is a satisfaction that easy can never give you!

CHAPTER 10
POST THAT

It used to be if you wanted to generate some buzz or promote your business paper was the only option. Business cards, mailers, fliers, brochures, fax transmittance, and letterhead were the primary method of marketing. Every now and then if you wanted to get snazzy (yes I said snazzy) you might splurge and purchase a radio spot or a TV commercial. Most of the time that was unreasonable because of the sheer amount of money involved. I have fielded many calls over the years from eager ad executives who want to sell time to me. They are armed with data and are definitely schooled in the craft of presentation. However, at the end of the day it was usually a no go because of the amount of money that was required to meet the demands of the contract.

With social media, all of that has changed. Money is no longer an issue and reaching people has never been easier. Think of the power behind entities such as facebook, twitter, and linkedin. With a few strikes of a keyboard you can instantly share information with people. This can be an incredible tool to promote your business.

However, this does not involve simply creating a facebook page that in turn floods other people's pages with endless coupon posts or useless updates. You need to determine the best way to use social media to promote your business. That can be tricky when there is a temptation to copy what other businesses are doing because it works effectively for them. If you copy them you will probably just end up blending in with the crowd and that is the last thing you want to do.

Now keep in mind, as I write this we have no corporate facebook page; nor do we have a regular twitter feed or a Northeast Pharmaceuticals blog that turns the corporate business world on its ear. Our industry does not necessarily dictate that type of marketing, but there are still ways we could use these tools more effectively and we are working on that. In the next few pages I hope to give you some creative ways to employ these devices that will in turn grow your business. Buckle up, let's ride.

First, let's address what the proper use of social media might be for your particular business. No matter what your business does, there is a universal quality to using social media that goes far beyond, marketing, branding, or public relations. I believe it can be summed up in one simple phrase, "engage the customer".

I have a friend named Brent Reynolds who owns a chicken wing restaurant in Alabaster, Alabama. It is called the Wing King. He has a facebook page. Go like his page on facebook right now before you continue reading. Better yet, go buy his chicken wings right now and thank me for the experience later. He does a phenomenal job with his product. He does just as good a job of managing his facebook page for the Wing King.

Brent will post coupons, discounts, and make contest announcements to his customers via his facebook page. He also posts pictures of events and recognizes customers publicly for their loyalty. In turn, he creates dialogue which turns into community. Facebook is not merely a means to "get the word out" about the Wing King, it is a way to interact with the customer. It is a way to involve them and engage them. It gives them a voice and a platform.

I think that is the one crucial element that most corporate entities totally miss when they go about using social media. If they come from an older generation they try to fit it into an old marketing scheme. In other words they use it in the same manner they would use the traditional marketing methods. This does nothing but frustrate the customer. Eventually, it will run them off and all the posting and tweeting in the world will not get them back.

So how do you prevent this from happening? You do what Brent did. You use social media as a means to engage the customer. If you own a restaurant like he does you might want to offer regular coupons that are only available to people who like your page or subscribe to your twitter feed. If your business does something totally different you will want to find other ways to engage the customer. You might use social media as a way to update customers on industry trends from time to time. You might want to preview new products or use it as an informal survey before you make a decision to roll out a new product. You might give the customer a voice. Let them vote on new logo designs or narrow down new product offerings. Whatever your business, use social media as a way to engage the customer.

Second, use social media as a way to engage your employees. Notice I said "engage" and not "spy on" your employees. I know people in various companies who friend employees on facebook or follow them on twitter just to see what they are up to. That is absolutely stupid. If you have nothing better to do with your time than play facebook police or twitter tattletale then your company will certainly pay for it in areas of morale and productivity. What you have done is create an issue in the area of trust. You have postured yourself toward the people who work for you with a "big brother" attitude and as a result your bottom line will reflect it.

Instead, you should engage your employees in a positive manner. There are endless ways to do this with social media. Maybe they did something outstanding this week and deserve to be recognized. If so, use it as a means to brag about them. If you know they are going through a tough time you might use social media to encourage them. You may never know the full impact of what this will mean, but the gesture will only take a few seconds out of your day. What have you got to lose?

You can also recognize birthdays, graduations, spousal promotions, or other milestones of importance. The possibilities are endless, but the results are almost immediate. I can almost guarantee you that your business will be more productive and profitable if you use social media to engage your employees in a positive manner.

The reason is quite clear. People are more creative when they are in a good mood. Having you reach out to them in a positive manner improves unity among the team and boosts morale. These are things you can not put a price tag on, but in my opinion they are essential for growth. Satisfied, productive employees do a fantastic job of serving even the most demanding customer. Use social media to engage. You will not be disappointed.

Another powerful use of social media is networking. You likely have people in your network who know other people working in similar fields or industries as yourself. Mine these contacts for other connections. You never know where a new connection might lead! When you network with like minded people you might come across some industry best practices you were not familiar with before. These new found efficiencies could increase your bottom line by reclaiming time or speeding up production.

Those connections could also lead to conference invites, partnerships, or new growth opportunities. All of those contribute directly to your bottom line. You also build up a certain amount of clout as you begin to make new connections. It won't be long before people start coming to you as a go to resource for industry happenings. When that happens you can smile because you know you are officially in the loop!

In addition to the items mentioned above, you might also find a a pool of new hire candidates who are perfectly suited for positions you have in mind as you grow and expand. Think of what this means to you. No more paying for costly ads or spending time posting ads online. All you have to do is tweet, make a post, or put out an update that says you are hiring. You make connections and people send qualified candidates your way. How much easier could it get?

I would like to make one other cautionary suggestion as you begin your foray into social media marketing. Remember that the internet is forever. How you present yourself online will make a lasting impression. If you post drunk pictures of yourself or make derogatory comments that is fine... you just won't work for me. I can not tell you how many party people have asked me for a job and then made the mistake of befriending me on facebook or connecting on some other social media platform.

After a glance at their profile and postings, the job offer ship sails quickly out of port. Nothing wrong with someone having a good time, but if that is all I see; I wonder if I can take them seriously. I wonder if they will take their job seriously. I wonder if they can manage their own life. Don't short change yourself by being too free spirited online. It will cost you in the end.

A final thing you can do to make a lasting impact online is provide workshops or links to other events that might further your employees in their career. It is important to remember that your online presence is two sided. There is the customer to be concerned with, but there is also the employee. Giving employees a chance to make positive comments about your corporate events is absolute gold. It is one thing for them to make a positive comment on your individual page (I am close to a lot of my employees); however it is another thing entirely for them to post "Best training session ever!" on their page. You can not put a price tag on that type of PR. It is good for morale when employees can generate buzz about your company to other people.

You see with Northeast the thing we forget at times is that some of our employees are an island. We operate in several states and there can be an assumption that everyone has the same opinion of Northeast because they all understand the company equally. We have to remind ourselves that many of them do not know anything about us unless we spend time with them. Giving your employees a chance to speak positively about your company in front of other coworkers is always a great thing. Consider creating opportunities online to do this by making posts about group training sessions or conference events and then allowing the employees to comment on them afterward. You might be surprised at the results.

So who knew diving into the online world could be just as broad as it is deep? Maybe all you were doing up until this point with social media was making an occasional post about your kid's eating habits or your dog's sleeping pattern. You never considered the fact that you could use it as a means to an end. Now you know better.

The information I just presented might seem a bit overwhelming at first. Go back and read this chapter again. Digest it. Let the information marinate. Process it thoroughly because one thing is certain; social media is an incredibly powerful tool. You must be familiar with it and know how to use it in today's corporate world. Use it well and you strike gold, misuse it and you strike out.

CHAPTER 11
KNOW WHERE YOU ARE GOING

So at this point in the book it is tempting to paint an unrealistic picture. I would love to tell you all things come up roses, everyone is enchanted with what we do, and we all live happily ever after with minimal amounts of struggle and hardship. Most people tend to think that when you "make it" things continue to snowball in your favor. Success churns out more success; so on and so forth.

However, nothing could be farther from the truth. It seems that now our problems are larger and they multiply quicker. The irony is that this has happened because of our success. Pharmacy issues that used to pop up on a quarterly basis now pop up monthly or weekly because we have 8 pharmacies instead of one. Customer care issues have multiplied exponentially. This happens when you move from servicing hundreds to thousands.

Success has arrived, but it comes with a price tag. Oddly enough, it has to be managed as well. Most people are used to managing problems. They are accustomed to managing tangible parts of business like employees, expenses, equipment, and the like. However managing success is a key component to running a business. Failure to do so could result in running your company into bankruptcy.

How could this happen? Well without a plan to manage your success you might expand too quickly and run into cash flow issues. When operating capital wears thin it does not matter how much money you are GOING to make. That number quickly becomes irrelevant when making payroll and paying other bills become problems. Who knew success could be such a monster?

Here is another common problem that comes as a byproduct of success. You become a target. Those who once considered you as harmless now put laser sights on your company. Take the following example from our story.

For several years we were able to fly under the radar at Northeast as the mental health market remained virtually untapped. No one seemed to notice us as we went around and signed up facility after facility. Our primary method was to attend the annual mental health conference in Birmingham, Alabama and set up an exhibitor booth. We would collect leads and handout tons of packaging samples and brochures (remember the previous chapter mentioning trade shows?). This went on for three years. That third year was a wake up call for us. We had grown substantially as a result of the business generated by the conference.

I vividly remember Don and myself setting up that year. We had a banner printed up that read "Northeast Pharmaceuticals. Proudly serving..." and what proceeded was a list of the mental health facilities we serviced. One of our competitors went to our booth after hours and wrote down the list of every mental health facility on that banner. Then they proceeded to call on those accounts and try to persuade them to cut ties with us and do business with them.

Our customers told us some of the things they mentioned and it was quite comical. Everything from promises of pharmacy grandeur to outright smear tactics were used to try and persuade them to make the switch. I am pleased to report that they were unsuccessful in their attempts. Not one of our accounts switched over to this particular competitor. Keep in mind that at the time we serviced just under half of the mental health centers in the state. Don and I joked that the next year we would make it easier by printing up a typed list to give them and save them the trouble of having to write down everything.

The point of the story is simple. Once you grow and gain traction you become a target. We had doubled or tripled in size every year since we purchased the business. For three years we were perceived as the new kid on the block. That fourth year we were a viable threat to the competition and they started to fight back.

So it is with the price tag of success. You have to learn to manage your success if you want to keep using that word or else you will find yourself using other words like negative cash flow, lay-offs, cut backs, etc. That is not a fun place to be.

So how do you do it? How do you manage success so it continues to drive your momentum and grow your business? The easiest way is to simply know where you are going. If you set the course for your company then managing success becomes an easy thing. Decisions are easy to make when you know where you are going. Profitability increases when you know where you are going. Exploring new markets is exciting when you know where you are going.

Knowing where you are going is somewhat of an art and somewhat of a science. It is like being an ancient mariner. You have to be able to set the course for your ship and also know when to make course adjustments as obstacles appear along the way. This is something only you can do. It is also something you must do.

Everything good and bad that happens in your organization is a result of leadership. I believe that wholeheartedly. It is a statement that carries a lot of gravity. It is sobering and provides a lot of focus for me as a business owner. If everything rises and falls on me, it is imperative that I set the course for my business.

This course creates focused, productive employees who perform their job with excellence. It also fosters a spirit of creativity by defining the creative area. It gives team members a chance to come up with ideas that further our goals and tap new markets. Know where you are going and set your course for success. What this has meant for Northeast can be summed up in the following quote...

"The best is the enemy of the good".

French Philosopher Voltaire

There have been many times that we thought we might pursue new markets or create other divisions of our company. In the end we have decided to let Northeast be Northeast. That decision has been very difficult when the grass has looked greener in other markets; but we have never regretted our decision to specialize in mental health. We know that market better than most. We have developed strong relationships in the industry, and as a result we are a go to resource anytime something new comes across the horizon with budget cuts or third party changes.

You will be faced with these same types of decisions. There will be many times, and I emphasize MANY times that other pursuits might seem like a good idea. In the end the decision will be left to you to decide if they are worthwhile or not.

At times that can be appealing. Especially when you are successful. It is easy to think that the success you have in one area will translate over into new ventures as well. Nothing could be further from the truth. You need to look at every angle, play out scenarios in your mind, do your homework, and make an informed decision. In time they will become easier.

For us the unspoken mantra is "Let Northeast be Northeast". If a new pursuit means that Northeast will flourish and grow we will go for it. However, if it requires too much of an investment into the unknown or has the potential to throw off our focus as a company we will always say no. If you want to continue to be successful, learn to manage your success.

CHAPTER 12
SOME TIPS AND TRICKS

This chapter is going to be somewhat of an off-road adventure. Following are some things I do when I approach a potential customer and pitch Northeast. Use this as a go to resource if you find yourself stuck in a negotiation or unsure of how to navigate a particular deal. These have worked well for me over the years.

One of the first things I try to do is find a connection to the client. I look around the room at what they have hanging on their walls, I look at the items on their desk. Are they a fan of a certain sports team that I like? Did they attend the same university that I attended, or better yet a rival school? If they have a degree on the wall do I share the same field of study or something similar? Do they have pictures of their kids littering their desk? If they do, I talk about mine. Are there any accomplishments or awards they have that pique my curiosity? If so, I ask about those things.

One thing I particularly look for is any military service memorabilia. This could be a medal that they received or a picture of their father or grandfather in a dress uniform. When I see that I jump on it. Not because I am trying to manipulate the conversation; but rather, because I love talking about my grandpa and Pearl Harbor.

His boat was attacked by the Japanese kamikaze pilots and one third of his ship, the U.S.S. Sigsbee, was blown apart. It had to be towed into port for repairs. He lost several good friends that day. It was a frightening event for him and a sobering realization that we were at war. If he had been standing 20 feet to the left, we would have lost him in the blast. It is a great story and I get to brag on my grandpa who is one of my heroes in life. Who would not want to do that?

The point of all of this is I am trying to make a connection with the client. Something that makes my world and their world more familiar and less foreign. The thing to keep in mind is you must be genuine if you use this approach or they will peg you as a manipulator from a mile away.

I ask about these things because I love to hear people and their stories. I ask because I want to know what makes this person tick. People display things in their office for different reasons. There is always one commonality though. They are conversation pieces. Don't deny them the opportunity of making conversation. It tells you a lot about who they are, what is important to them, or what they are passionate about. This ultimately tells you the type of person you will be dealing with and that is very handy to know. All of this begins with making conversation, or making a connection over something they have in their office.

Another thing I live and die by is the following rule... never take a contract into a first meeting. Now there are countless other books that may tell you otherwise, however for me it is absolutely useless. I think it is quite presumptuous to expect someone to look over a contract and sign it when they have only met you one time. Not bringing a contract to the first meeting does a couple of things.

For one, it allows you to get to know the customer and understand their needs. Every contract (or service agreement as we call them) that I have ever taken to a meeting has required some sort of modification with the exception of one. Why? Because every account is different in one way or another. A standard contract will not cover every service nuance. Don always asks the potential client in our first meeting for a list of "perfect world" expectations that the customer has concerning its pharmacy. We then take that list and address each expectation accordingly. Then when we present them with a contract, all of their expectations are addressed within.

The second thing it does is foster communication between me and the client. In my mind the relationship with the customer begins at the first meeting so any opportunity I create to get in front of them again strengthens that bond. Not bringing a contract to the first meeting does just that.

I get another chance to interact with the client. I get to ask if they have any more questions since they have had some time to process (which they usually have); then I schedule another meeting so we can discuss things further. What I am creating is a history between us. The more I am in front of the client, the richer the history. The richer the history, the deeper the relationship. That is the same with any relationship if you think about it. No one ever brings wedding vows with them on a first date!

Here is another great tip to keep in mind if you want to foster a long, healthy relationship with your customer. I learned this one early on from one of our first accounts. I remember it well.

We had just decided to open up our pharmacy in Montgomery after a disastrous first year of business. Our morale was low, but we were on a mission. The mission was simple. We had to get accounts quick to pay for the new pharmacy or our entire company would implode and shut down rather quickly. We were definitely in a "run rabbit run" frame of mind. As a result we began making cold calls in Montgomery, Prattville, Wetumpka, and Millbrook.

As it happened, we landed an account in Prattville that I made mention of previously. They are still with us today. Part of that reason is because the leadership and staff have committed to grow with us on our journey. They have grown about as much as we have grown (funny how success usually teams up with success huh?). Working with them has been a pleasure and we appreciate their business.

Yet there was one incident that sticks out in my mind from one of our first meetings with them. They were using a pharmacy that had this horrible medicine on a roll system that is supposed to be easy and convenient. The system works as follows.

You get your medicine in a box according to the following time schedules, AM, Noon, Evening, and PM. If you take medicine at all four times then you get four boxes that each contain a month's worth of medicine. Inside the boxes are little pouches with pills in them that are connected together to make one extremely long strip. At 8 am the customer goes to the box, reaches in, tears off a pouch, and takes the medicine. At noon the same thing happens again and so on and so forth. Sounds relatively easy and convenient.

In my opinion it is neither. The head nurse shared the same opinion for the following reasons. She would get medicine shipped to her that she had to check for accuracy before the consumer could take it. That meant she had to go through each box, unroll the strip of medication, and count them to make sure the correct amount of doses were in the box. She then had to make sure the correct amount of pills were in each pouch. If something was incorrect she had to ship it back and wait on the correct box to return. All the while she was hoping the consumer would not run out of medicine before she received the box with the corrected doses.

We told her we were local and could make med changes as needed. Also, our cards are packed with a weeks worth of medicine instead of a month. This means that she could still receive a month's worth of medicine, but she would only have to check a week at a time for accuracy if she chose to. We also told her that she would have a dedicated person in the pharmacy that she would deal with.

I will never forget her response. She seemed shocked that we would go to all of this trouble to meet her needs. She told us that she had not received one visit from the current pharmacy that was servicing her. That floored me. Why in the world would you not want to visit your customer? That is your lifeline. Without them you don't exist.

We decided after that meeting to step up our game and visit our customers regularly. That meant we would visit them every three months to get the relationship where it needed to be. After that we would follow up periodically and ask the all important question... How are we doing? We decided not to hide behind voicemail or email. We were going to know our customers. We were going to be accessible and visible. If you want to go far, do the same. Make a plan now to visit your customers regularly. You will be glad you did.

Let's change gears for this next tip. So far I have given you some tips on how to get to know your client; ways to foster communication, make connections, etc. Those work well for people who are wired up in a normal manner. You make a pitch, create a few opportunities to get to know them, submit a contract, volley a few changes back and forth, and presto!... you have a new customer. However, there are some occasions when you have to deal with difficult people.

You know the type. People who live to make everyone else's life a living hell. People who are constantly abrasive. They thrive off of conflict. They breath fire. They love to make children cry. They hate puppies. They voted for George McGovern for president. You get the point. These people are what I call "opinion heavy" and "content light". Selfish to the core with an ego the size of a hot air balloon.

I love dealing with these types. You may think I am kidding, but that is a serious statement. I may not look the type, but I am a calculating, competitive sort. People that know me will tell you I thrive under pressure. I can make things happen when deadlines are imminent; and I have created many exit doors where there were supposed dead ends.

I am good at what I do. As a result, if you are heady or ego-driven, I will absolutely own you at the end of the negotiation process. I will make more money off of your account than you thought possible while you think you are getting a good deal. I don't do it to be obtuse, I do it because you are a jerk. I am going to compensate my company's bottom line. It's only fair right? We are going to have to deal with you for a while so I make sure the experience is profitable.   Seeing the profit generated from your ego ensures I will smile through all of the "complaints", "threats", and "fits" you will throw.

So what is the secret to dealing with these types?   The answer is quite simple. Play chess not checkers. Ego driven people always approach negotiations with one goal in mind; they want to see what they "get out of it". They could care less about growing their company.   Instead, they want to make themselves feel like a shining star.   As a result they play through negotiations like a game of checkers. Their whole objective is to "beat" you. It is a race to see who can get to the other side and wipe out their opponent the quickest.

So again, you play chess while they play checkers. That's what I do. I let them play their silly little game and actually let them "win" in their mind. The whole time they are trying to run their game, I am playing mine with a bigger set of rules and a larger scope. They are boxed in and don't even realize it.

There are several different ways to do this. The primary method is by way of our contract or service agreement. If I have been dealing with a real head case of a CEO, feel free to substitute other words of choice for "head case", then their contract looks totally different than the standard one I give out. There is much more "wiggle room" built in to give them something to argue with me about. It is nothing more than a distraction to keep them from looking closely at other sections.

You know, the sections where our interests are protected to ensure our profit margin is secure and growing.

All you are doing is redefining the boundaries. Let's take the example down to brass tacks. If you know a particular CEO has a reputation for being aggressive with pricing to the point of driving the price ridiculously low then let them. Rewrite your contract to allow for some adjustments and heated discussion. Then when you arrive at the final price it will be exactly where you want it to be. The CEO feels great because their ego is stroked, and you can smile internally because you ran your game and won!

There are a million other little things you can do to make an impact. Things that indirectly affect productivity and ultimately your bottom line. Congratulate employees for their hard work whenever you see them. Call customers and ask their opinion of certain contract points when working your next deal. Send out random emails to clients with updates on what your company is doing and where you are headed. Thank your customers often for their business. Reach out to them on facebook and twitter. If you really want to get down to details, send a card on their birthday or a handwritten note telling them what their business means to you. Hire a person who's only job is customer retention and watch what happens to customer morale. All of these things make a difference to your bottom line. I know because they have made a difference to our's.

CHAPTER 13
THE WORKAROUND

Sometimes you do your best and it is simply not good enough. You do your homework, put on your game face, bring your "A game" and still get yourself handed back to you on a platter with all of the trimmings and a nice gravy boat. Those are some of the worst times you can imagine. Yet I believe they are necessary. They force you to come up with new ways to solve the problem. I remember a few times when my best was not good enough.

Most notably was the time I made the decision to go to LAMP. Now for those of you who do not know it, LAMP stands for "Lanier, Academic, Motivational, Program". Lanier was the high school where the program was based. Think magnet school for the gifted and you have it right. It was a nightmare for me. Now that sounds like I had the worst experience of my life there, but nothing could be farther from the truth. I made friends and had a great time socially.

However, academically it was a nightmare. I consider myself to be smart. You know above average intelligence and the like. I never struggled in elementary or middle School to get an A on my report card. I could "See spot run" and do long division with the best of them. It simply was not a challenge for me. As a result I was encouraged to enroll in LAMP at the end of my 9th grade year. Most of my friends were going there so it seemed like the logical thing for me to do as well. I would fit right in.

Negative ghost rider. That first year I had to actually study to get a B, much less an A. It was a four year struggle to do what I was able to do previously with my eyes closed! I hated homework, loathed certain classes, and got that knot in my stomach when the teacher would call on me in class to answer a question. It was real work!

At first I thought that maybe I just needed to work harder and study longer to get good grades. I tried that and it was a miserable failure. I really put in the time and all I could seem to muster were C's. I remember having this momentary bout of panic as I realized that my best was simply not good enough. I did not know what I was going to do, but doing nothing was not an option.

So what was my answer? Innovation. See we were told in our interview process that most of the teachers would give us homework as if they were the only subject we had to contend with during the week. This meant that on average you would have a minimum of 3-4 hours of homework a night. Yes ladies and gentlemen per night, NOT per week.

That being said I conducted a little self-assessment. I was grasping the concepts in class, but my grades were slipping because of homework. It was killing me! So I made friends quick and we did a homework workaround. We split up questions in history and chemistry, we divided up math problems and passed answers around in the morning before class. We even had big parties where we would try to get ahead with our homework in certain subjects where the teachers taught straight through the text book. We turned homework into a system and mastered it using a workaround.

It was at that point in my life I learned a lesson. Difficulty forces innovation. When you think about it that is true with most any situation in life. I know with Northeast we do not get creative with anything until money gets tight. When that happens paper clips get counted, trash bags are put on back order, expense reports are scrutinized, and rebate contracts get looked at. Everything is reined in to make our operation as efficient and waste free as possible. It should be that way all the time, but that is not the case. Funny how difficult circumstances can foster efficiency and innovation.

So let's bring Northeast into this example. It's about three years into our business and we are actively pursuing our niche market of mental health. We are actively targeting our home state of Alabama and as a result are aggressively marketing to every mental health center in the state. Enter Montgomery Area Mental Health. An enigma of sorts if you will. We are servicing mental health centers in the northern part of the state and the southern part of the state. Yet we live in Montgomery and have been unable to even schedule a meeting with the Mental health center in our own hometown. I know this because I am the guy who tried to schedule the meeting.

It was like trying to meet with the prime minister of China. I could not get around the gate keeper to save my life. The executive director was always either out of town, in a meeting, or just plain unavailable. I might as well have been calling the Tonight Show trying to speak with Jay Leno. This went on for about a year.

Then one day we stumbled across one of their group homes in Montgomery. I say we because I can not remember who discovered it. I just know it was not me. That is beside the point though. We were going to try a workaround and see if we could slip in through the back door. Even though our chances of getting in were slim, we were going to try anyway. We approached cautiously with baited breath.

We scheduled a meeting with Sharon Roeder who was actively involved in managing part of that facility at the time. We went over our packaging options, other services we could provide, and how we could make a difference for them. She loved what we had to say! She loved it so much in fact that she encouraged us to schedule a meeting with Henry Parker who was over the whole group home.

We did that and he loved what we had to say. That turned into a meeting with the elusive administrative staff and they LOVED WHAT WE HAD TO SAY! Contract negotiations ensued and we began servicing them in a few weeks. I am so glad we did not let the difficulty stop us. I am so glad we did not give up.

This was more than a case of being persistent paying off. Being persistent would have gotten us nowhere, I am convinced of it. We could have called and tried to schedule a meeting for years with no luck. No this was a case of getting creative and implementing the workaround.

There will be times in your own career where you will have to do this. You never know when it might happen or what the circumstance may be. It could be that you are trying to go for that job and need to find a way to gain audience with the CEO to explain why you are the best option. Find the workaround and use it. You might be faced with trying to make your business profitable and think you have exhausted all measures to do so. Find a workaround and use it. There is always a way to get to your goal. Just because you come up to a barbed wire fence right before you cross the goal line is no reason to stop and admit defeat.

Remember, anything worth pursuing is worth attaining. Don't let silly roadblocks keep you from your dreams. Find a way to get in front of the right person. Find a way to get around that pesky gatekeeper. Come up with something to raise your profit margin and cut expenses. Find the workaround. Defeat is not an option. There is always a way.

Back to Montgomery Area Mental Health. We found the workaround and used it. We proceeded with our usual implementation. We started with one group home and folded in other group homes until we were meeting the demands of all of their residential business in about two months. From there we moved to their shot business, which in turn led to their outpatient programs. We have had them as a customer for about three years now and have enjoyed every minute of it! However, here is the odd thing about all of it.

It was a full three months into servicing them that we met the executive director. I say we because Don met him one day on a delivery. It would be another few weeks until I got to meet him. Talk about irony! We were already making money off of the account and I would not have been able to pick the executive director out of a lineup if you paid me. Makes for a nice ending to the story though.

It also proves that there is something to be said for being tenacious and using the workaround. Especially when you know you can make a difference to the customer. There is no reason not to! So go for it. The only thing you will gain by not attempting is lost revenue. Who wants that?

CHAPTER 14
ALL OR NOTHING

Over the years we have made many presentations. Sometimes I am amazed at what the selling point is for the customer. You know what I am talking about if you have been in sales for any length of time. You go in with a preconceived notion of what might get their attention in the sales pitch. The pitch is carefully prepared and orchestrated because you have done your homework and know a lot about the potential customer. So you blaze a trail forward. You make the pitch, and at the height of the presentation when you have them really interested; you make a point to mention the particular product or service that will make the most difference for them. You wait for them to bombard you with questions, but instead it is cue the crickets time.

I can not tell you how many times that scenario has played out with me. What I think is the best selling point for the customer turns out to be something they are totally uninterested in. Why is this the case? At the end of the day you must remember that any sales job is a people business. Yes there may be a product or service you offer that would really be a great fit for their organization, but in the end it is the person saddled with the job of producing for the organization that is looking for their world to be changed. Never forget this fact.

For us that person is usually a nurse or clinical director. They are usually not present at the first meeting. The first meeting usually consists of an executive director and a CFO. Sometimes a few residential coordinators are present to offer perspective on the service aspects of what they do.

That meeting is all about saving the facility money or saving them time which in turn will save them money. This is a language the executive director and the CFO understand. If things go well there we will schedule a second meeting where a few key people from their operational staff will be present. These people are usually the director of nursing or clinical director as well as a few other nurses. These are the people we have to make a difference for. They are actually in charge of the consumer's medication and deal with it on a daily basis.

As a result their pains are far different than the CEO's. They could care less about saving money. They are looking to save time or make things more efficient. They have a lot to do in a day and patient medication is only one part of it. They usually have a lot of influence over which pharmacy the facility will choose and most of the time the executive director will let them make that decision outright.

So with that said you must always remember to sell the whole product. You never know what will "click" as a selling point so make sure you have given them everything to look at. The first few times we made a presentation we focused on what we thought would be an important selling point to the customer. We were met with a less than enthusiastic reception. Then we would begin to explain other free services we offered and they would jump all over it!

Over time that response began to make sense. You have to understand when we first purchased Northeast the two sisters who owned it were not charging for anything. They did not charge for packaging, printing medication records, delivery, or after hours services. Northeast Pharmaceuticals made money by billing the insurance companies for the patient's medicine. That was it. We saw no need to change any of that so we continued the practice when we purchased the company. Plus, it felt so good to tell potential customers that our services were free.

Another thing happened about the time we purchased Northeast. The practice of nursing changed somewhat for the state of Alabama with the installment of the Nursing

Delegation Program. Essentially what this program did was put restrictions on what non-skilled nursing employees could do with medicine for patients at certain facilities. These happened to be the types of facilities we serviced.

The non-skilled employees are not nurses, but work closely with medicine that the patients receive. The program made sure that only nurses were able to make authorized changes to medication and placed certain handling restrictions on what those employees could and could not do as it pertained to medicine,

One of the ways the program did this was through compliance packaging. No longer could a facility have a bottle of medicine laying around for a patient. All of the patient's medication had to be packaged in some sort of blister pack or other approved packaging material. This would make it easier for the staff to identify if the medicine had been compromised. It would also make it easier for the patients and the non-skilled staff to see how much had been taken.

Over the counter items also had to be packaged accordingly in some sort of compliance packaging. Up until this point most facilities had a big stock bottle of Tylenol and other over the counter type pain relievers that they used for all patients. The Nursing Delegation Program changed that. From now on any over the counter medication had to be patient specific. This meant that we had to place those things in some sort of compliance packaging as well. They had to be patient specific and had to be identified as such.

There were many other changes that the program made, but those were the only changes that really affected pharmacy practice. For us however, these changes were no big deal. We already packaged medication in compliance packaging. In fact we had several different types of compliance packaging. The only change up part for Northeast was now we had to pack things like Tylenol in cards for specific patients. This meant we actually made a little bit more money since now we were billing out ten or twenty doses of Tylenol per patient instead of charging the facility for one stock bottle to use as needed.

Now enter the local pharmacy. These guys have been going about business as usual for years. They stand behind the counter and fill prescriptions as people walk in. They also fill prescriptions for a few mental health facilities in the area. Life is good. Then the Nursing Delegation Program happens and they get a phone call or a visit from the clinical director informing them that all medicine must be packaged in some sort of compliance packaging. The local pharmacy says "No problem", but since the packaging is an extra expense he will have to incur he solves that by passing it on to the facility. So he or she fills the medicine in compliance packaging and charges the facility $5-$7 per package to do this.

You can probably see where this is headed. This was one of those times in business where the stars aligned for us beautifully. We had not charged for services from day one. Regulations around the industry changed, but they changed in our favor. You can not fault the local pharmacies because they charged for providing compliance packaging. In their minds it was a new expense.

To us it simply meant more business. We went around for a few years and scooped up new accounts because the pharmacy the facility was using started charging for packaging. All we had to do was tell facilities that we did not charge and they were ready to sign up.

I well remember the first time this realization dawned on us. We were making a pitch to a facility in Alabama and had hit all of the high points in our mind. We told them how we would set them up on a cycle fill to make managing medication easier. We told them that we would not do any late night deliveries. All of their deliveries would occur during normal business hours. We told them that they would get to choose their start date and that we had back-up measures in place should they need something after hours (sometimes patients have a slip and fall or get an infection that requires a trip to the emergency room. We have ways of getting them medicine should that happen). We pitched all of this and the facility was rather unimpressed because their current pharmacy was providing those same services.

Then it happened. They asked what our prices were for packaging and for printing off medication administration records. Don and I kind of blinked at each other and he quickly replied "There is no charge". The nursing staff could not believe it. All of a sudden the discussion turned from " We are perfectly happy with the services we currently receive from our local pharmacy", to "I can't believe we have been paying X amount per month for packaging! When can we start?".

From that moment on we would make our pitch and wait for that question to be asked. The point of all of this is simple. We made assumptions that other pharmacies were not charging for packaging as well so in the beginning we did not mention that fact on our end. We were so busy trying to "compete" with the competition that we did not tell all of our story. Once that light bulb came on though, we never neglected it again!

You should not either. Always make sure you tell your potential customer ALL of what you can do or you may leave that presentation with the same amount of their business you had before you walked in... NOTHING. We have picked up accounts many times over the years for several reasons that to us seem like minor ones. People make the decision to choose us because we do not charge for packaging, we do not charge for medication administration records, and we do not charge for delivery.

We have also had people choose us for the strangest reasons. My favorite story is from an account we serviced in

Montgomery. They were a 60 bed facility and Don had a tie to the director. He had actually worked with her husband at another job. We went in there thinking we were a shoe in. Nothing could have been further from the truth. We made the pitch and waited to be asked for a contract. Instead we were politely told that nothing was broken and therefore it did not need to be fixed. They were going to stay with the local pharmacy they were using because they had a great working relationship.

We left there chuckling. I remember kidding Don about how much good it did us for him to know her husband. We had been optimistically hopeful and now that ship had sailed. They would continue doing business as normal and we would call on them again in six months or so (we always do that, no never means no, remember?).

Then a funny thing happened. That ship sailed right back into port on Monday morning and docked at our front door. Don called me very excited saying that they wanted to switch over and use us. I went in to the office and began drafting a contract for Daniel to review. What was the reason for the sudden change of heart you ask? Well as it happens, over the weekend they needed to get an antibiotic for a patient who went to the hospital. The pharmacy charged them fifty dollars for delivering the medication to them. That was the straw that broke the camel's back. She called Don throwing a duck fit ready to start service with us as soon as possible.

The only reason she was able to make that decision was because we shared ALL of what Northeast could do for her. Had we left out the part about free delivery and free after hours services we never would have gotten the call. That pharmacy was already doing everything else we were doing so there really was no reason for them to switch over. The weekend delivery tipped the scales in our favor.

Allow me to go down a rabbit trail for a moment. We took that whole experience as a lesson in business ownership. We always made note that the local pharmacy lost the entire account over a fifty dollar charge. We commented to each other that if we went in to their pharmacy and gave them a fifty dollar bill to buy the account that would never work. They would laugh us out of the store. However, that is essentially what happened. We never forgot that.

CHAPTER 15
NEW HORIZONS

So what does the future hold for Northeast? I can not be sure. Right now I feel like Miles Standish must have felt when he took the Mayflower across the ocean to the new world full of hope and promise. They fought incredible odds, but in the end that bump into Plymouth Rock paid off.

This is much different from our friend Christopher Columbus who discovered the new world. He too fought a few obstacles to get where he was going. For one he had to gain support. He approached Portugal, Venice, Genoa, and the British crown before finally obtaining funding from Ferdinand and Isabella of Spain. The reasons for rejection varied. Most notably, Portugal turned him down because they thought he had underestimated the mileage to what is now Japan. That meant the trip would require more money so they scrapped it. Other countries were dealing with different political pressures or points of focus so he was not even given audience to present his proposal.

Imagine the frustration of having a dream and coming up against roadblock after roadblock. The mental stress must have been incredible. To actually be successful Columbus had to be one persistent guy. His persistence paid off. He received funding and charted a course for the new world.

And what a journey it was! An adventurer at heart, he set out to find new trade routes for the Spanish Empire. A common misconception is that people thought the world was flat. The reality is only a few people at the time thought the world was flat; most of those with Columbus knew better. It was merely a legend to tell at night around a lantern while eating dinner in the ship's hull. He dealt with some mild mutiny at times but overall the trip was smooth sailing.

He ended up making four trips to the new world and making a fortune for the Spanish empire. However, in the end he found himself at odds with Spain and was placed under house arrest until his death. He even tried to sue the monarchy unsuccessfully for 10% of the trade profits with the new world. They of course rejected his suit rather handily. Their reason for rejecting him was simple. Since they had relieved him of governorship they did not feel obligated to honor his contract. After he died his relatives continued, trying to sue on his behalf in a series of suits called the "pleitos colombinos". They too were unsuccessful.

Now compare that story with Captain Miles Standish who came to colonize the New World. He was a separatist with a mission. Remember, the separatists were not interested in reforming the English church. They were content to leave that futile effort to the reformers. The separatists thought that the church was too far gone. They desired to move away and establish their own movement. So with backing from a financial group called the "Merchant Adventurers", the Mayflower expedition to the New World was born. This would be an endeavor of colonization rather than establishing trade. England even supported the effort. I mean think about it, what would be the harm in letting a few upstarts do their own thing (and all the hard work) while you reap the reward in taxes?

So they made the trip and the fact that you are reading this proves it was successful. We colonized and prospered! That first winter was rough and I am sure there were many times when they had doubts, but they made it through in spite of everything. We are here today because of that.

The question though is this... why was the English colonization effort so successful while the discovery effort never gained much traction? The answer is simple. Columbus was on a mission to "get" something. Standish was on a mission to "start" something.

I don't think you can ever underestimate that subtlety. If you run your business (or even live your life) to merely "get" something you will achieve it every time. You will "get" something. It may not be anything fulfilling but it will fill you for a moment and that feeling can be deceptive. You should be on a mission to start something. It boils down to a difference of looking at the weather versus looking at the horizon.

Some of you know what I am talking about, but for those of you that find that statement a bit fuzzy, let me explain. When you look at the weather and notice a storm you immediately size up the situation. You go through your options and determine whether you should leave or stay.

When I lived in south Florida hurricanes would blow through from time to time. The local news outlets would make you think the world was coming to an end. You had to make a determination as to how dangerous the storm was and whether or not it merited your departure. Once I remember leaving and fleeing to the other side of the state. You were excited because you felt like you had beaten the competition. The storm was coming and you dodged it.

Another time I remember opting to stay because the storm blowing through was a category one. That was my first time riding out a hurricane and it was scary. Winds were sustained at 70 mph and there was a lot of rain. My friend's neighborhood flooded and we ended up walking to his house in waist deep water. It was a harrowing experience. We made it there only to find the inside of his house sitting in three inches of water. That may not seem like a lot, but he and his wife lost wedding photos, heirlooms, and anything that had wooden legs because it was all standing in water. They went through a difficult time after that, but I am proud to say that today they are doing better than ever. They survived!

For me the experience was different. We went to the store and stocked up on batteries, bread, water, and other essentials. My daughter Chloe was still an infant so we grabbed diapers and the like. I made another trip to the hardware store for plywood. I came back, drilled out some peep holes, and screwed the wood to the house windows to protect from flying debris. Inside we stacked up furniture on top of other furniture that we thought we could sacrifice if flooding occurred. Then we left and went to a friend's house to ride out the storm.

I remember thinking at the time that it was exhilarating. I was going to beat the storm, protect my family, and save our belongings. I felt quite accomplished with myself afterward. All of the preparation had paid off. We survived and were free to go about our lives.

What a nice story right? Consider this. Not once during that time did I ever stop to think about what I was going to do with the rest of my life. I never thought about where I would be in ten or twenty years. I never considered what my 401k options should be, if I wanted more children, what type of business ventures to pursue, etc. None of that ever crossed my mind. I was too busy beating the weather.

Now that analogy is not perfect, but I think it translates well. In business you must remember that weather is temporary. You will have things happen that will drive you nuts. For us there are constant changes to pharmacy regulations as well as regulation changes with the facilities we service. We adapt to those as we should. Sometimes it takes a while to work through it, but we do.

There is a lot of satisfaction when you adapt to the change and maintain profitability. There is a high that carries over giving you a sense of accomplishment. You begin to believe that you have really done something. All you did was manage the weather.

If you keep doing that you will lose sight of the horizon which in turn will cost you business. If you lose sight of the horizon, the colony never gets established. As a result new horizons will never be discovered. Managing the weather is necessary. Just don't let it become your focus and make you stagnate.

So back to the question that opened this chapter. What is on the horizon for Northeast? The landscape of pharmacy is changing. Automation is becoming more commonplace and the old ways of processing prescriptions are giving way to new electronic measures. Our customers are being pushed to go paperless with government incentives and the like. Paper medical records will turn into electronic records and this should in turn cut down on waste and save them money. It is a good move. It has forced us to move in that same direction.

This has opened up a new horizon for us. Now we have other products to sell not just to our existing customers, but to potential new clients as well. It is exciting! With changes in other long term care industries, new markets may open up for us. There are certain markets we have purposefully stayed away from because of their cut throat nature, but the horizon paints a different picture now. We might be open to pursuing those and colonize that area as well!

The point in all of this is the main idea of the entire book. Keep your eyes focused on where you are going. I can not stress that enough. Always keep your eyes focused on things in front. If something looms over head, you can drive under it. If it is in your way, drive around it. If the weather fogs your vision, turn on your wipers. Just remember to always keep your foot on the gas and drive the bus forward!

EPILOGUE

Life is curious. As I write this I am going through one of my most difficult times as an individual. My mother is in the hospital with a brain tumor. She is scheduled to have it removed soon. We are told she will be fine after recovery. That information still gives little comfort beforehand. The unknown is always greater than the known.

I have heard that statement before, but my friend Larry Hart reiterated it to me just the other day. He summed it up like this. Think about a horror movie. They always start out so creepy. They are full of suspense and designed to set you on edge. Most of the time the monster/demon/entity/killer is not revealed until the end.

In the meantime, your mind has conjured up a picture of what this thing might be. Then the "thing" is revealed and the movie instantly becomes less scary. Why? Because you have lifted the veil of the unknown. Once you are able to see something you can size it up. Once you are able to see something you can create a plan of action. Dealing with the known is always easier.

It is the unknown that can drive you mad if you let it. The unknown strips you of rationality. It attacks your morale and towers over you like a menacing giant. It can affect your health by creating worry, depression, and severe anxiety. It will master you if you let it. I am convinced that it knows this even though the unknown is purely an abstract concept.

The only way to deal with it is to fight back. Don't let it lord over you or plague you with it's haughty nature. Confront it. Attack. Choose to lift the veil. You will be glad you did. Whether it is personal or business in nature, you will be glad you did.

So with that said, it has been my pleasure sharing these stories with you. I have many more so that means more books. In the meantime my blog at jasonwbritt.com will keep you in the loop concerning future developments. I like to laugh so prepare yourself to be entertained at times. I can also be found on facebook.com/therealjasonbritt and on twitter I am @jason__britt if you are interested in following me. I wish you the reader all the best.

ABOUT THE AUTHOR

Jason Britt currently lives in Montgomery, Alabama. He enjoys spending time with family and friends, playing guitar, and an occasional scotch.

Appendix

Fox, Jeffrey J. *Secrets of Great Rainmakers:The Keys to Success and Wealth*. New York, NY: Hyperion, 2006.

Trump, Donald. *How to Get Rich*. New York/Canada: Random House, 2004.

Trump, Donald. *Think Like a Billionaire: Everything You Need to Know About Success, Real Estate, and Life*. New York: Random House, 2004.

Trump, Donald. *Trump University Wealth Building 101: Your First 90 Days in the Path to Prosperity*. Hoboken, New Jersey. John Wiley and Sons, 2007.

Trump, Donald and Zanker, Bill. *Think Big & Kick Ass in Business and Life*. New York, NY. Harper Collins, 2007.

Maxwell, John. *The 21 Irrefutable Laws of Leadership: Follow Them and People Will Follow You*. Nashville, TN. Thomas Nelson, 2007.

Maxwell, John. *Developing the Leader Within You*. Nashville, TN. Thomas Nelson, 1993.

Maxwell, John. *Thinking for a Change*. New York, NY. Time Warner Books Inc., 2003.

Kiyosaki, Robert. *Retire Young Retire Rich*. Printed in the USA. Plata Publishing, 2002.

Gladwell, Malcolm. *The Tipping Point: How Little Things Can Make a Big Difference*. Printed in the USA. Little, Brown and Company, 2000.

Gladwell, Malcolm. *Blink: The Power of Thinking Without Thinking*.

jasonwbritt.com

www.ingramcontent.com/pod-product-compliance
Lightning Source LLC
Chambersburg PA
CBHW051335170526
45166CB00002B/830